AN INSTANT PLAYSCRIPT

UGLY
RUMOURS

TARIQ ALI AND
HOWARD BRENTON

NICK HERN
BOOKS
London

An Instant Playscript

Ugly Rumours first published in Great Britain in 1998
as a paperback original by Nick Hern Books Limited,
14 Larden Road, London W3 7ST

Ugly Rumours copyright © 1998 by Tariq Ali and Howard Brenton

Tariq Ali and Howard Brenton have asserted their right to be identified as the authors of this work

Cover image: courtesy De Wynters

Typeset by Country Setting, Kingsdown, Kent CT14 8ES
Printed and bound in Great Britain

ISBN 1 85459 426 5

A CIP catalogue record for this book is available from the British Library

CAUTION All rights whatsoever in this play are strictly reserved. Requests to reproduce the text in whole or in part should be addressed to Nick Hern Books

Amateur Performing Rights Applications for performance in excerpt or in full by non-professionals in English throughout the world should be addressed to the Performing Rights Manager, Nick Hern Books, 14 Larden Road, London W3 7ST, *fax* +44 (0) 181 746 2006, *e-mail* orders@nickhernbooks.demon.co.uk

Professional Performing Rights Applications for performance by professionals in any medium and in any language throughout the world should be addressed to Casarotto Ramsay, National House, 60-66 Wardour Street, London W1V 4ND.

The publication of this play does not imply that it is necessarily available for performance by amateurs or professionals, either in the British Isles or overseas. Amateurs and professionals considering a production must apply to the appropriate agents for consent before starting rehearsal or booking a theatre. **No performance may take place unless a licence has been obtained.**

Ugly Rumours was first presented at the Tricycle Theatre, London on 22 October 1998. Press night was 2 November 1998. The cast was as follows:

POLLY MENDACITY	Jaye Griffiths
THE CARDINAL	Richard Durden
CHERRY-POP/CHARLIE FARRAGO	Carla Mendonca
TONY-BOY	Neil Mullarkey
MRS THATCHER/MRS WINDSOR	Sylvia Syms
GORDON MACDUFF	Gordon Kennedy
MEDIA BARON/JOHN SMITH	Tony Selby
SIR MALVOLIO CLAPPER/ JACK COMPOSITE/BIGGLES/JOSPIN	Owen Brenman

Directed by Christopher Morahan and Stephen Rayne
Designed by Bunny Christie
Lighting Designer Jenny Kagan
Sound Designer John Leonard

The play takes place in a very real world.

CHARACTERS

TONY-BOY	A Prime Minister
POLLY MENDACITY	His spin doctor (played by a woman)
CHERRY-POP	A Prime Minister's wife
GORDON MACDUFF	A Chancellor Of The Exchequer
CHARLIE FARRAGO	His spin doctor (played by a woman)
THE CARDINAL	A Lord Chancellor
MARGARET THATCHER	A corpse
JOHN SMITH	A ghost
MEDIA-BARON	A media baron
SIR MALVOLIO CLAPPER	A fashionable man of film and theatre
JACK COMPOSITE	A union leader
BIGGLES	A rising business man
JOSPIN	A French Prime Minister
MRS WINDSOR	A constitutional monarch

Throughout the performance the headings of the scenes are shown on a running digital display about the stage.

On every seat of the auditorium there are two focus cards: a green YES card and a red NO card.

SCENE ONE

MY NAME IS POLLY MENDACITY AND THERE IS NO REASON NOT TO DO WHAT I SAY

Dark stage. Spotlight on POLLY MENDACITY who wears a slick black skirt with a long slit up the thigh. He is played by a woman. She wears a nineties gender-ambiguous outfit suggesting style without content. She has a mobile phone and a pencil moustache.

POLLY.   (With menace.) Good evening. Each and every aspect of this theatre is now fully under control. I know what you're thinking, don't, I am not a control freak. Say to yourselves: she is not a control freak. I hope all mobile phones are switched off. Please turn pagers on vibrator mode. (With great menace.) This is going to be an interactive evening.

(A PAUSE. She switches to charming mode.)

Those of you who've paid to enter this theatre by credit card are now all safely registered at Millbank. Thank you.

The socially-challenged amongst you who paid by cash have been filmed by our security cameras and the tapes will be sent on to the Inland Revenue. The art of modern politics is not knowing how you all live, but where you live.

My name by the way is Polly. Polly

	Mendacity. I used to be the Policeman without Portfolio, the genius who won the last election. (PAUSE. A naughty look.) At last my talents are being recognised. See! I rise and rise. Today I am the Secretary of State at the DTI. The Department for Treachery and Influence. And tomorrow . . . who knows? You don't. I do. (Suddenly stern.) But just get one thing straight. I run all the shows in town, including this one and the jury's still out.
	(Flirtatiously.) By the way do you like this moustache? Or should I take it off? (With menace.) Ready with your focus cards. Please concentrate, this is a democracy. All those in favour of my moustache, please raise the green YES focus cards. All those who hate my moustache, please raise the red no focus cards.
	(POLLY does the opposite to what the audience vote. Unknown to Polly a Cardinal creeps up behind him and pinches his bottom. POLLY squawks.)
CARDINAL.	No more juries. Hoi poloi. Law too complex. Chums on the bench know best.
POLLY.	That was the Lord Chancellor. A merry soul and an early riser.
	(The CARDINAL shoots back on.)
CARDINAL.	Civil servants in at 6am. Self in office 7am. Navigate ship of State. First aperitif, noon. Lunch 1pm. Day over. Next thing I know. Civil

servants in at 6am. Self in office at 7am. . . .

(The CARDINAL wanders off. A loud scream is heard from the darkness behind. CHERRY-POP in pink nightie is sitting up in bed, petrified.

Heading: BEDROOM SCENE.)

CHERRY-POP. I saw her again.

(Tony-Boy, in a Princess Di T shirt showing her in her land-mine outfit, sits up and looks at CHERRY-POP.)

TONY-BOY. (Shiftily.) I don't actually think there's anyone Cherry. I do take you seriously, but I do promise you there's no one else here. Trust me.

CHERRY-POP. Tony-Boy, I saw her and so did you.

TONY-BOY. (Testy.) You can't have because I told you didn't and you didn't because she's not here. I am entitled to this agenda. It's my agenda.

CHERRY-POP. My God you'd be terrible in a witness box. I am going to continue the cross-examination.

TONY-BOY. Polly hasn't paged us yet. Go back to sleep.

CHERRY-POP. You go back to sleep, don't you dare talk to me like that.

POLLY. (Into his mobile.) Unspun. It's an unspun scene. Stop this. Stop this now. Lights out. (Back-stage goes dark.) Ready to spin. Spin.

(Scream of delight. Lights on.

Heading: BEDROOM SCENE – SPUN.)

CHERRY-POP.   (Yawning deliciously.) I had such a lovely dream Tony-Boy.

TONY-BOY.   (Smiling to audience.) Tell me about it, darling Pop-Pop.

CHERRY-POP.   I dreamt she was here in our bedroom, looking at you longingly and you know something, Tony-Boy, I wasn't jealous at all.

TONY-BOY.   I think it's only fair to tell you darling that Margaret *is* here. She never left.

(The GHOST of MARGARET THATCHER walks across the stage. She is carrying a strange extractor contraption, like a car Hoover.)

THATCHER.   You know I'm always right. Here's my head and heart extractor. (Working the pump.) It pumps even the tiniest bit of socialism out of the body. Doesn't John Prescott look wan and pale in a lovely suit these days? Lots of people have had it done to them and they're the better for it. Pump carefully three times daily and, I promise you, there will be no turning back.

(They wave to her cheerily. She EXITS pumping. Suddenly they both squawk.)

TONY-BOY/CHERRY-POP.
            Did you pinch me?

TONY-BOY.   I didn't pinch you. Do you believe me?

CHERRY-POP.   Fifty percent of me does. Thirty percent of me doesn't and twenty percent of me doesn't know at all, Tony-Boy.

TONY-BOY.   Oh my god. That's the lowest rating you've given me this year. (To audience.) I hope this is a suspect sample, don't you?

(The CARDINAL appears out of the bed.)

CARDINAL.   Lord Chancellor. Ship of state steady. Good new judges. Swollen in the face, freemasons. In the year two thousand and twenty-six I might even give you a black Attorney General. I am a great reformer.

CHERRY-POP.   It's such fun being in bed with an unwritten constitution.

(THE CARDINAL disappears. Official wake-up call.)

Don't get out that side of the bed, Tony-boy. Feng-shui.

(TONY-BOY and CHERRY-POP jump out of bed and waltz off the stage. There is a cacophony from next door: banging and screams.)

POLLY.   (Aside.) Don't panic. Noisy neighbours. The Chancellor of The Exchequer doing his early morning wake-up exercises. How puny those muscles are under those crumpled suits.

SCENE TWO

NOISY NEIGHBOUR

GORDON, a Chancellor Of The Exchequer, is lying on a bed having a nightmare. He has gone to bed partially undressed, top of a suit, no trousers. The bed is very messy with books,

9

socks, official papers, a kilt, files, red boxes etc. He thrashes about.

GORDON. I know not why this thing is yet to do! Euro Euro, not Japan, no! South Korea General strike, no! Ecu, ecu, echo . . . The nightmares of economic history . . . Marx Keynes. Ah! Adam Smith! Too too radical. I recede into endless vistas of recession. (He gets out of bed and begins to sleep walk.) Where's the door? My office. Number Ten. Rightfully mine. Stop recession.

(ENTER CHARLIE FARRAGO. He is played by a woman.)

CHARLIE. (Aside.) I'm Charlie Farrago. Contrary to what Polly Mendacity has told you, I'm the one who runs this show. (Indicating GORDON.) He's my boy and we control the money, they can't move without us. (To GORDON.) Gordon, recession!

(GORDON wakes with a start.)

GORDON. Don't do that to me Charlie. An abruptly aroused Chancellor can damage the economy.

CHARLIE. Boss, let's clear this mess up.

GORDON. Don't you touch it. This mess is awaiting a review.

CHARLIE. You told me to wake you early for our secret inspection of the Dome.

GORDON. Yes. The Dome. It spoils my dream like a poisoned potion. How are we getting there?

CHARLIE. I thought we'd hire a boat, just to fool MI5.

GORDON. Charlie you little bundle of joy, you think of everything.

CHARLIE.	(Aside.) I do. I'm indispensable to him. That's why the lot next door never stop trying to get rid of me.
	(They EXIT.)

SCENE THREE

POLLY changes into a suit, humming a tune which she begins to sing lightly to herself.

POLLY.	(Sings.) Yesterday, power seemed so far away (Speaks.) But now it has come to stay And I believe Oh yes, I believe in Nothing Nothing but power. (And to the audience.) And . . . don't pay any attention to Charlie Farrago. She counts for nothing, her days are numbered. (With menace.) Even listening to her could damage your careers.
	(TONY-BOY is maniacally brushing, then flossing his teeth throughout this scene. He is before a small Conran type mirror and basin.
	Heading: THE PM'S DAY TODAY.)
TONY-BOY.	Polly. Pretty Polly. Come on.
POLLY.	Wrong shirt. Tony-Boy. Swizzles on television.
TONY-BOY.	Not on Sky.
POLLY.	Everything looks good on Sky. No content.

TONY-BOY.	Remind me. How many days from today is the day when we have the day of the next election?
POLLY.	One thousand two-hundred and thirty-eight.
TONY-BOY.	Good. That's one day less than it was yesterday. Get the simple things right I always say, and the complex things will sort themselves out.
POLLY.	Very nineties.
TONY-BOY.	Polly, is it a House of Commons day today? I do hate going there. Too many fragrant babes sitting behind me. And Prescott's aftershave.
POLLY.	No not today. Half an hour a week is enough.
TONY-BOY.	Yes, I am running the country.
POLLY.	We are. But it is a day of tough choices.
TONY-BOY.	Oh good. What am I doing?
POLLY.	Usual stuff. Neutralise treasury. Suck up to business. News massage session in the rose garden.
TONY-BOY.	Funny how quickly one gets used to it.
POLLY.	But, big, big, one Big problem of the day . . . meeting the Media-Baron. Euro-Referendum?
TONY-BOY.	Do I have to Euro today?
POLLY.	(Sternly.) It's a Euro must.
TONY BOY.	Can't I go back to Ireland? I love walking on water. I really do. I just

	found myself doing it naturally. Like winning the election.
POLLY.	Have you forgotten that neurotic Polaris submarine that shadows your every move? Gordon?
TONY-BOY.	(A reverie.) Isn't it time to decommission the Polaris? Buy something more up to date from the Americans? (Out of the reverie.) Next?
POLLY.	Democracy check. Focus groups. Millbank reports a rogue group in Doncaster.
TONY-BOY.	Rogue?
POLLY.	We collected them at Tesco's for a joint meeting with the Sainsbury's focus group, but lost them when we were transferring.
TONY-BOY.	Could they have gone far? Have they stopped liking me?
TONY-BOY.	They've not escaped to Scotland? That'll be the third group we've lost in three months.
POLLY.	Forget them. We're fine where it matters. Surrey is up to 92 percent.
TONY-BOY.	Good. I always knew Surrey was creative, compassionate, outward-looking. I believe in the British people living in Surrey. (Mood changes.) Now let's look at the dark side. What's the Opposition doing today?
	(This section will be continually updated.)
POLLY.	Ken Livingstone is campaigning to be Mayor of London. He's doing a striptease today at the Windmill.

	Roy Hattersley is addressing the ungrateful dead at the Groucho Club on the need to take the railways back into public ownership.
TONY-BOY & POLLY.	Cuckoo! (They giggle, stop giggling.)
POLLY.	The Foreign Secretary is discussing ethical punishment beatings with the Saudi Ambassador. After which he is attending a lunch honouring ethical white mercenaries in Africa. (A PAUSE. With menace.) But bad Gordon news. His gloomy Highness The Chancellor of the Exchequer is threatening to visit the Dome.
TONY-BOY.	(Starts. Stares into the mirror.) That's too much. Stop him.
POLLY.	I'll try, but we must be careful. His ego is the size of a water melon. This makes him ultra-sensitive.
TONY-BOY.	Polly, how did it come to this? Did I do something wrong?
POLLY.	You took his job.
TONY-BOY.	Oh I see. I do sometimes wonder whether Gordon might have made a better Prime Minister than I. The answer comes, but I do wonder. (A PAUSE.) I shouldn't let my judgement be conditioned by colleagues who like him less than I do.
POLLY.	That's my job. Treachery and influence. I make sure everyone's so busy loathing each other that they all have to say they like you.
TONY-BOY.	It's at times like these I really do feel you're indispensable, Polly.

	(They look at each other. They kiss.)
POLLY.	Right. First up you're booked in for one hour. Communications skills with Sir Malvolio Clapper.
TONY-BOY.	Not that again.
POLLY.	Polly's rule: polish and polish and polish again. Shine. Shine perfectly in the sun.
	(TONY shows his teeth.)
TONY.	I do think in the digital age people notice teeth.
POLLY.	Neil never understood teeth, that's why he lost. Media loves dental floss. The smile is now perfect but what if there's a war Tony-Boy? We need the war-look. War in the Gulf, War in Serbia, War in Scotland. War. War. Serbia, Iraq, Scotland. War. Scotland. S.N.P. Europe. Media-Baron. War in Europe. Mauritius tests H-Bomb. You've got to be prepared.

SCENE FOUR

WHO HAUNTS THE DOME OF DOOM?

Outside the Dome. Gloomy dawn. Enter the CHANCELLOR OF THE EXCHEQUER with CHARLIE in a boat. CHARLIE, played by a woman, is aggressively power-girl dressed.

GORDON.	Pour on rain on Dome. Kind rain. Drown wicked Dome. Modish monument to a twisted vanity. Thames' turbulent water melt this evil Dome. Contaminated soil.

CHARLIE. What else lies buried beneath the ground? This is where Polly hides the bodies. See that buoy? That's where we dumped redistribution of wealth. See that radioactive glow underneath the ground? With the genetically deformed dandelions on it? That's where we buried social justice.

GORDON. I am the man to put this right. But I'm only a son of the manse. I mood, I brood. Why am I spending more and more money on my hair?

(Enter the ghost of JOHN SMITH.)

GHOST. Remember me?

GORDON. (Startled.) Who are you?

GHOST. Wax desperate with imagination, Gordon.

GORDON. (Startled.) John Smith. The ghost of Leader past.

CHARLIE. (Aside.) What's this, fate? Spinning fate is hell.

GORDON. The best Prime Minister we never had. Why appear to me?

GHOST. I was most foully murdered. Climbing my Scottish mountains I was most cruelly modernised.

CHARLIE. S'cuse me, what's with the chains?

GHOST. They are the chains of compromise.

GORDON. Oh my prophetic soul. But gentle ghost, tell me something. What did you think of my last budget?

GHOST. Horrible, horrible, most horrible.

GORDON. But was it not bravely done? It was

	a redistributive budget. It's just that the rich didn't notice.
GHOST.	Nor did the poor. Shun the luxurious discomforts of the rich, Gordon. Remember, I was most foully murdered.
GORDON.	What do you think of welfare-to-work?
GHOST.	Remember full employment? Remember socialism?
CHARLIE.	Don't reply Gordon!
GHOST.	You are the last hope of those who built our great movement. I don't wish it to be said that the party that was born with Keir Hardie died with John Smith.
CHARLIE.	Did, didn't it?
GHOST.	See the day breaks. I sink back beneath this Dome.
GORDON.	Gentle Ghost, just before you go. What is this Dome for?
GHOST.	What did Tony-Boy tell you?
GORDON.	It makes us cool. It's fun. It's interactive.
GHOST.	Wrong. Not cool. Not fun.
GORDON.	Then what is it for?
GHOST.	Beware the interactive digital democracy promised by media monsters. (PAUSE.) Is it true that you're getting married?
CHARLIE.	Shut yer gob.
GHOST.	Who is this creature so dangerously near Government?
GORDON.	Poor world's been turned upside

GHOST. down since you died, Ghost.
We all have creatures like this now.
Pity the living dead.

(The GHOST fades away.)

They who only go half way dig their own graves. Remember Frank Field.

(He has gone.)

GORDON. That unnerved me, Charlie.

CHARLIE. All that was once solid, Gordon, melts into air. In the nirvana of the global economy only recessions are real.

(ENTER POLLY.)

POLLY. (Aside.) Right, come on, focus time. There was that word in Charlie's mouth and how horrible for that word to be there. The R word. (Whisper.) Recession. (Aloud.) But recessions can be good for business. Not industry, real business. Making money. I mean how else can we get a cheap pool of unemployed workers? Only the arseholes, the total failures, jump out of windows because they raided the pension funds. A recession is like a fat free diet, it makes you lean, and extremely bad tempered, and very fit. I hope my message is . . . trickling down to you.

All those convinced that Tony-Boy can handle a recession, raise green focus card YES.

(Ignores any result. Does not call for the NO vote.)

It's wonderful how he keeps ahead of you all.

(She EXITS, answering mobile.)

SCENE FIVE

CHERRY-POP POPS A QUESTION

Enter CHERRY-POP.

CHERRY-POP. (Aside.) I'm just an ordinary person. Like so many hard-working QCs who can't quite make a million a year, and there are lots of us, I want to work, look good, shop, but power sometimes gets in the way. It affects everything. Power haircuts, power shopping, power breakfasts. Is power good for me, is power bad for me? What is power? Where does it really lie?

(She produces a divining rod. It trembles. She follows the power of the rod and EXITS.)

SCENE SIX

MEDIA TRAINING SCENE or HOW TO BE SINCERE

A knocking on the door.

POLLY. Show time. Emergency communication skills.

TONY-BOY. Oh I do hate the arts.

POLLY. So do I, but these are popular arts. Arts without a social agenda, like Oklahoma.

	(POLLY gestures off. ENTER SIR MALVOLIO CLAPPER, a fashionable film/theatre producer/director.)
	Prime Minister, this is Sir Malvolio Clapper.
CLAPPER.	(Excited.) Good morning Prime Minister. Good morning Polly. I support Spurs, is that all right? (Lowers voice. To POLLY.) Does he know we lunch?
POLLY.	No.
TONY-BOY.	Do call me Tony-Boy.
CLAPPER.	Gosh. Safe.
POLLY.	(Whisper.) Boots.
TONY.	Do you want me in my cowboy boots?
CLAPPER.	If they work for you.
POLLY.	They do.
CLAPPER.	The art is in the image. It's what people see that really matters, not what you do. It's wonderful to be part of the civilised hypocrisies and bland deceits of politics.
	(They stare at him.)
	Too radical? Sorry.
	(POLLY throws a pair of cowboy boots onto the stage. TONY-BOY pulls them on enthusiastically.)
POLLY.	Mrs Cherry-Pop!
	(ENTER CHERRY-POP with a little Priapic African god around her neck.)
CHERRY-POP.	Oh *hello* Mello. Say hello to Da-da.

CLAPPER.	Oh you've got a Da-da. I've got one too. I wear mine round my waist.
CHERRY-POP.	Da-da keeps away the evil spirits.
POLLY.	(To CLAPPER.) Time is money. Get on with it.
CLAPPER.	Screen test time? Family smile.
	(TONY-BOY and CHERRY-POP give a big family smile.)
	Cherry-Pop a touch – are you knowing what I mean – of the professional woman with earth mother in there? Think of your knickers being a little too tight, it'll help.
	(The sudden flash of her photograph smile.)
	Tremendous.
CHERRY-POP.	Da-Da wants me to go now. I've got to be at the Old Bailey. I'm defending that rather amiable serial killer from Cheltenham.
CLAPPER.	Tremendous. I mean awful. (A moment's hiatus.) OK it's a wrap for you.
	(CHERRY-POP goes off.)
	Anything need a pecial polish?
POLLY.	Do you mind?
TONY-BOY.	Actually, there is something. I'm going to have to do something I've never done before. Annoy some people and convince others.
CLAPPER.	The trouble is, your audience don't know what they like, they like what they know.
TONY BOY.	Yes that is the problem. You see, presentationally what I need to do is

	to go with the grain, but also tackle negatives. How do you do that on stage and screen?
	(SIR MALVOLIO CLAPPER is in deep thought.)
CLAPPER.	Always the nightmare. Truth versus the box office. The trick is to make them so happy they don't notice. Like the Full Monty.
TONY-BOY.	Should I take all my clothes off?
CLAPPER.	Save that for the recession. Now. You're going to have to project. There are two ways of doing this.
TONY-BOY.	Oh great.
CLAPPER.	The method. Marlon Brando. Al Pacino. President Clinton.
TONY-BOY.	How does that work?
CLAPPER.	You have to make yourself believe in what you saying and doing. Deeply. In your heart.
	(A PAUSE.)
TONY-BOY.	What's the other way?
CLAPPER.	The English method. Irony. Pissing in the audience's eyeballs in such a way that they love it.
TONY-BOY.	Oh, politicians know all about this.
CLAPPER.	You see, you've got to learn to be a bit of a tart.
TONY-BOY.	Really?
CLAPPER.	Yes. Some of our greatest actors are very big tarts.
TONY-BOY.	Gosh. I thought they were all androgynous.

CLAPPER.   That too. (He pushes on.) You see,
                  all that matters is what seems.
                  You've got to project sincerity.

TONY-BOY.   But I am sincere, actually.

CLAPPER.   People don't necessarily know that.
                  If you're not seen to be sincere,
                  what you really are doesn't matter.

TONY.   I see. It's . . . (A gesture.) . . .
                  gestural. Could there be a third way
                  of acting? I mean, could one project
                  an idea where none exists?

CLAPPER.   The greats do it all the time. It's
                  just like pretending to be upset
                  when someone dies. Like Mark
                  Antony in Julius Caesar. (Sucking
                  up.) I'm told your Mark Antony at
                  school was brilliant.

TONY-BOY.   But I really was upset when John
                  Smith died. (Voice cracking.) It's
                  cruel to suggest I wasn't. I was . . .
                  my heart broke.

CLAPPER.   There. You did it! That's it!
                  Sincerity. Now. Are you focused?
                  Centred? The Chi-lines balanced?
                  Give me your Churchill.

TONY-BOY.   'We shall fight them on the
                  beaches.' That's too conflictual. We
                  must meet them as they come up
                  the beaches. We must go down the
                  beaches with some fluffy towels.
                  We shall never surrender.' No.
                  Better is 'We will negotiate all night
                  until they all fall asleep.' We will
                  negotiate all night and Polly will
                  put it on the news before they
                  notice.

CLAPPER.   Off-text, I think. (With faded
                  dignity.) I quote Cicero. 'One needs

23

	a grounded knowledge of the most varied things, so as not to rattle off meaningless words for others to mock at … '
TONY-BOY.	That's a bit tricky, I'm not a professional you know. I'm just the bloke doing the job.
POLLY.	Time's up.
	(POLLY gives CLAPPER a brown paper envelope.)
	I have an idea for you. Some lobby firms, because of general malice and ill-will, have recently lost their credibility. Why don't you set up a new one? Give individual arse licking in the arts a more solid institutional basis.
CLAPPER.	(Dreamily.) Yeeeeeees. I'm there. We could call it AFTA. Arse Licking For The Arts.

SCENE SEVEN
GORDON'S AGONY

GORDON.	Charlie, do I have to get married?
CHARLIE.	Yes.
GORDON.	Can't I go to a monastery? Why should I be a breeder of sinners?
CHARLIE.	Let's get two things straight Gordon. One, the media needs a wedding. Two, she'll breed, not you.
GORDON.	Who's going to give me away?
CHARLIE.	The Governor of the Bank of England.
	(They EXIT.)

SCENE EIGHT

DISHING IT OUT – MEET THE MEDIA BARON

Cabinet Room in No. 10. TONY-BOY, CARDINAL, GHOST of THATCHER, POLLY. THATCHER is drinking.

TONY-BOY.	Now look, now look Margaret. You're frightening Cherry.
THATCHER.	I always found that when I put my face near people, it unnerved them. (She nears TONY-BOY.) Especially men.
TONY-BOY.	(Steps back.) We agreed the bedroom was out of bounds. Cherry's a modern young woman, you know. She's the only one here with a real job.
CARDINAL.	Lawyer? A real job? (Laughs.)
POLLY.	The deal was you stayed in the cellar.
CARDINAL.	But she's the ghost in our machine. We need her.
THATCHER.	We agreed I could come up whenever the Media-Baron was expected. What I always found so attractive about him was how the hair on his wrists stuck out from under his cuffs.
CARDINAL.	(Looking under his cuffs.) I know what you mean.
TONY-BOY.	I, I think we can handle him ourselves now.
THATCHER.	Oh I don't think you can.
POLLY.	I had dinner with the Media-Baron's daughter everyday last week. She said he was charming. I found her charming. He said I was charming. I found him charming.

	They're all charming. It's a charming family. Power transforms and absolute power transforms absolutely.
	(They muse.)
TONY-BOY.	It really does, really.
THATCHER.	What surprised me was that the strangest men began to lust after me. Like Isaiah Berlin and Christopher Hitchens.
CARDINAL.	Power has a wonderful bouquet. Like a Chateau Petrus.
POLLY.	(Aside.) Six hundred quid a bottle. All is show.
THATCHER.	Power becomes you. You're doing really well Tony-Boy. But son of Margaret? No, no, no. You must become more radical and conservative.
TONY-BOY.	These terms. They don't mean much any more. I mean. What I mean is we're beyond left and right. There are no enemies in politics. Politics is conflict free now. I feel like killing people who don't realise that.
POLLY.	Just those we've buried.
TONY-BOY.	It's a third way forward.
THATCHER.	I only needed one way.
	(A helicopter noise is heard.)
POLLY.	(On her mobile.) Good, good. We're ready. Secretaries to position. Marksmen to rooftops. Total security blanket in force. It's the Media-Baron.

	(All kneel as MEDIA-BARON ENTERS. Musak plays and stops.)
TONY-BOY.	Welcome, Media-Baron. I am proud and privileged to stand before you ... (He is in reality kneeling.) ... as a new kind of Prime Minister of our country.
MEDIA-BARON.	One cross on the ballot paper, one tabloid headline and a Nation reborn.
TONY-BOY.	If everyone agreed to agree then agreement would always be possible.
MEDIA-BARON.	In this post-modern world, there is always more than one narrative, Tony Boy.
POLLY.	(Whispers.) You're upsetting him. Press pause and rewind.
MEDIA-BARON.	Get this eurocrap off my brogues now. There's nothing else to discuss.
THATCHER.	I agree.
MEDIA-BARON.	What's this out of date old bag doing here? Get rid of her. Print workers and Prime Ministers come and go.
THATCHER.	I am still in power. This country is in my shape.
MEDIA-BARON.	Learn from me, drive your cart and horse over the bones of the dead.
	(A chilly moment.)
TONY-BOY.	Polly will take you back to the cellar now, Margaret. Put some fresh earth out for you.
THATCHER.	Whatever you do, wherever you go, you'll never get rid of my teeth marks in your neck.

POLLY.	(Leading THATCHER away.) Busy, busy, busy bee. That's me.
THATCHER.	(EXITING. Tottering on her bad feet.) Thank you, thank you, nice meeting you. Mustn't keep you any longer.
CARDINAL.	(to MEDIA-BARON.) Hello.
MEDIA-BARON.	Who's this big girl's blouse in pink?
TONY-BOY.	He's our Lord-Chancellor, Media-Baron.
MEDIA-BARON.	How I hate England. Flummery, ceremony, Buck House, men in white-stockings with buckles on their feet. So what d'you do? Use your wig to hide your big fat tits?
CARDINAL.	We are the Lord Chancellor of the United Kingdom. We are the lawmakers. We uphold its laws. I have the keys that turn its locks. I can open doors just as easily as I can slam them.
MEDIA-BARON.	Weekend in California?
CARDINAL.	I'll go and pack now.
	(He EXITS.)
MEDIA-BARON.	Talk me Euro in two minutes..
TONY-BOY.	(Smiling eagerly.) Well, to really modernise we must find something modern to join and that, no disrespect, means, means Europe. Actually if we don't go euro they'll all gang up against us and Britain will go bankrupt. And we'll have to tell people that, and in order to succeed we really do need your newspapers. No disrespect, but your very nasty paper, for which I often write . . .

MEDIA-BARON. Do you?

TONY-BOY. ... oh yes, yes, but could you make sure they don't attack me more than once a month?

MEDIA-BARON. Are you seriously talking croissants here?

TONY-BOY. Not just croissants, Media-Baron. I mean the Tuscan cuisine. Wild mushrooms risotto. Grilled peppers. Fresh garlic pulled from the earth at dawn, the dew still upon it. And the hundred and thirty-two different varieties of sausages from Germany and Austria. Paella from Spain. And France, Media-Baron. France. Truffle pigs. Paté de foie gras. An embarrassment de riches. The richest markets in the world, yours for the taking, Media-Baron.

MEDIA-BARON. All my papers are in sensible languages.

POLLY. (Aside.) English and Chinese.

MEDIA-BARON. Some of your advisers think of me as an unsophisticated yokel who can't change his Y fronts.

POLLY. We don't think that. We love you. You're the most powerful man on earth.

MEDIA-BARON. I'm coming to that. You see I understood even when I was in short trousers, that Keynes was bullshit. It was a cumulative squeeze on profits that broke the springs of investment.

POLLY. Oh God they go on like this at the DTI.

MEDIA-BARON. You failed. Anyway, tits always look better in a Union Jack.

TONY-BOY.	Media-Baron, you must understand. We are forging a new patriotism focused on the new potential we can fulfil in the new future. We must be modern and cool and forward-thinking and then we will go forward and up. Even though we disagree on Europe we have no choice but to agree. I mean . . . Can't we have the Euro, but not have the Euro? As a way of agreeing. (A PAUSE.) I mean we can't have politics breaking out. They have nothing to do with agreeing with me. THAT's the Third Way.
MEDIA-BARON.	Cut out the crap, Tony-Boy and find a way out of your Euro pudding.
POLLY.	(Whisper.) Change the subject!
TONY-BOY.	(Out of nowhere.) You know I often find myself reading the Old Testament.
MEDIA-BARON.	The Daily Telegraph?
TONY-BOY.	No, the real thing. Amos. Ezekiel. Job.
POLLY.	(Aside) Impossible to spin those geezers.
TONY-BOY.	And do you know, I often find things in the Old Testament which are exactly the same as what I'm doing.
MEDIA-BARON.	Yes. I've parted waters.
TONY-BOY.	Like the third way. God could find third ways. Like asking Abraham to sacrifice his son in order to save him.
MEDIA-BARON.	What was the Almighty up to with that one? (PAUSE. Chuckles to

	himself.) Abraham caught with ram in thicket.
TONY-BOY.	Let me get back on message. I see Europe as a giant Noah's Ark. You're Noah. The nations go in two by two.
MEDIA-BARON.	You mean the Ukraine, Poland and that Russian Zoo? That's not Noah's Ark, that's the Titanic.
TONY-BOY.	(Sweating.) There will be an upper and a lower deck in our Euro Noah's Ark, Media-Baron. And you'll be the Captain. And when the flood recedes the entire earth will honour you. You'll live for nine hundred and ninety years.
MEDIA-BARON.	Poofy, pillow-biter stuff this, Tony-Boy. I'll give you some Old Testament. This is my mother's milk of an Old Testament. I give you the seven plagues for England. I visited upon thee Wapping-style magazine supplements, Thatcher, a hail-storm of trade-unionists heads, Richard Littlejohn, the slaughter of all first-born socialists, drowning Man United in boiling oil . . .
POLLY.	That's only six plagues.
TONY-BOY.	What's the seventh?
MEDIA-BARON.	You go Euro on me, and I'll have the boys do a special one for you right out of the blazing eye of the Sun. You won't know what's hit you. Every day every second, every paper, tv station, on and on. You won't stand. Serial killers can't stand neither will you. You'll be surprised by the surprises I have in store for you. You'll lose more than

	your family's respect, your mind, your balls, your referendum. You'll lose your very sense of being.
TONY-BOY.	Are you threatening me, Media Baron?
MEDIA-BARON.	My satellite footprint hangs above your head.
	(The MEDIA-BARON EXITS.)
POLLY.	(Aside.) Can we afford to bury the Media-Baron and not to praise him?
TONY-BOY.	Polly! Do something.
POLLY.	I'll have to be careful. I'll just take a few precautionary measures. (Immediately on his mobile.) Conrad Black? Lunch tomorrow at your club. (Press a button.) John Birt? Drinks tonight at my place. (Presses a button.) Biggles? Call in your Euro chums. Time to balloon.

SCENE NINE

REVENGE SOLILOQUY

GORDON alone.

GORDON.	Now I am alone. How elastic our consciences have become. Those of us, that is, who possess them. No problems for Tony-Boy, he was blessed from birth. Born without consciousness of any need for a conscience at all. Teflon Tony. (A PAUSE.) Why do I mingle with bankers who make love to unemployment? Too much talk of recession unnerves me. If it comes firm action will be needed. Enough

of this. Look yonder at that bright sun in the shape of a Euro, see how it dispels the ugly clouds that threaten from the East. The bile bubbles and burns my throat! Tony-Boy, you are puffed with pathetic ambition and the trappings of power. You cling to the underbelly of an American president, feeding the vanity of the beast. Your special relationship with the Media-Baron – your tongue permanently ensconced in his forked posterior – has become a matter for mild concern. But events inform against you and events will bring you down. So contain thyself, dull revenge, thy time will come.

(EXIT.)

SCENE TEN

MILLBANK GYM – GOING FOR GOLD IN ONE UPMANSHIP

Millbank Gym, POLLY and CHARLIE are both working out while taking calls on their mobiles.

POLLY.	Charlie.
CHARLIE.	Polly.
POLLY.	What were you and Gordon doing at the Dome?
CHARLIE.	What is the Dome really for?
POLLY.	It is beyond your narrow, live-for-the-moment imagination.
CHARLIE.	You don't really know! You're running it and you don't really know!

POLLY. Avoid. Down that route trouble lies.

CHARLIE. You know I loathe you.

POLLY. Mutual.

CHARLIE. Look, this war between our masters is damaging the whole project.

POLLY. You mean Gordon's losing and you want a truce.

CHARLIE. It's just that it may be my narrow, live-for-the-moment mind, but haven't you noticed people are getting sick of us?

POLLY. People are getting sick of you, and people like you Charlie. Lowly spin doctors. I'm helicoptering upwards and upwards. Secretary of State. Member of Cabinet.

CHARLIE. This is why you're the most hated man thing in the country. don't get me wrong, I admire that. Polly, can I ask you a professional question without giving anything away?

POLLY. Try.

CHARLIE. What would we do if one of our kiddie-winks actually went off his trolley?

POLLY. Gordon hearing voices, is he, since the reshuffle? Needs to be sectioned?

CHARLIE. Leave it out! It's Tony-Boy we're all worried about. Turning the Media-Baron off. Thinking the only men who can run Government Departments are Supermarket Millionaires.

POLLY. Well the less members of the House of Commons in the Government the better. Part of the project.

CHARLIE. And ... (Lowers voice.) There's a whisper he's going to say Euro with a smile. Gordon needs to know.

POLLY. No he doesn't. A good Prime Minister never tells the Chancellor of the Exchequer anything before it's been cleared by the Focus Groups.

CHARLIE. C'mon Polly. The focus groups can't decide on the Euro. Cruelty to animals beyond all reason. You need the Media-Baron on side.

POLLY. Leave the Media-Baron to me. We're fellatioing him 'til he's blue in the face.

CHARLIE. (Deadpan.) It's a technique.

POLLY. What interests me is just who is Gordon talking to these days?

CHARLIE. Real people. Our people.

POLLY. You mean the ungrateful dead?

CHARLIE. I'm in denial on this.

POLLY. I have the video-tapes. Who is he talking to? There's a strange mist. MI6 are trying to enhance the image, but nothing.

CHARLIE. The people can't live on bullshit cakes for ever. My boy's got principles.

POLLY. I thought he was looking a bit peaky.

CHARLIE. Our policies are for the long-term.

POLLY. Gordon won't give up on the living dead, will he? All that old stuff is gone forever. Finished. Buried. Dead. Gone. Think fresh. Think new. We're not energy-sappers,

	we're energy-givers. You're too oppositional. Tell Gordon, no one's indispensable. We are all shufflable, underneath Tony-Boy's arm-pits.
CHARLIE.	Ugh. The funniest things turn you on, Polly. Is it true neither sex shaves in Brazil?
POLLY.	Do you really want to be Ambassador to Brussels? For the beer?
CHARLIE.	Bastard.
POLLY.	I hate Gordon.
CHARLIE.	I hate Tony-Boy. Gordon's more intelligent, anyway.
POLLY.	No he isn't.
CHARLIE.	Yes he is.
POLLY.	No he isn't. Tony-Boy walked on water.
CHARLIE.	Everyone walks on the Dead Sea.
POLLY.	Gordon gave our bank away. Gordon gave our bank away.
CHARLIE.	Anyway I get more publicity than you. I've had three profiles this month. Mail on Sunday. Sun. Times. And one Steve Bell to myself.
POLLY.	Three profiles? I've had 23 since we came to power. Two television documentaries. And twenty-five strip cartoons. And . . . and Harry Enfield's doing me on television.
CHARLIE.	How did you spin that?
POLLY.	John Birt's a friend of mine.

CHARLIE.   (Giving up.) You're so busy spinning yourself. You've forgotten how to spin Tony-Boy.

POLLY.   Oooooh, handbag! Right. Only one way to settle this one. Focus. Focus. Focus.

CHARLIE.   Hocus-Pocus.

POLLY.   Focus, folks. Would you like to marry Gordon or Tony? And men can vote. Green cards for Tony-Boy, red cards for Gordon. Go!

(Whoever loses says: 'Unrepresentative Sample.')

POLLY.   (To CHARLIE.) I'm not talking to you any more. Not now that I'm a Cabinet Minister at the heart of this Government.

CHARLIE.   Heart of the Government Polly? I think you've got the organ wrong.

POLLY.   I haven't.

CHARLIE.   You have.

POLLY.   Haven't.

CHARLIE.   Have. This truce is over.

POLLY.   Great! Stop the scene. I'm telling the story and this is how it goes: learn to fight; do it right; expect the worst; burn the bridges; pull together; show the way; massage the facts; seize the day; do it better; keep them guessing.

SCENE ELEVEN

GORDON MEETS THE UNIONS – EVEN HALITOSIS IS MORE IN FASHION

POLLY. (Aside.) The plotters are thickening. The Gordonites are meeting in secret tonight. You think you're clever, Charlie. You thought we'd never look there. Not in the Trade-Union Room in Madame Tussaud's waxworks.

(Dim Lights up on large motionless men in blue suits, only one of whom is real.)

LITTLE GIRL'S VOICE OFFSTAGE. Who are those men, mummy?

MOTHER'S VOICE OFFSTAGE. Once upon a time, in the industrial jungle, there were big bad men dressed up as wolves. They were called trade unions and they terrorised everyone. 'Til one day there came a lovely lady all dressed in blue and she was called Blue Ridinghood. And single-handedly she ate them all up.

LITTLE GIRL'S VOICE. But I like wolves mummy, they're kind.

MOTHER'S VOICE. Come away dear.

(Enter GORDON and CHARLIE.)

GORDON. (Whispers.) Are you sure you've got the venue right?

CHARLIE. Not even Polly would think of this. Hello Jack, pensioners' friend. Big Frank. Hi there Hughie – those were the days, eh, tanks on the lawn of Number Ten? Is that you Sapper?

	Television's changed now. Right, which one of you is alive?
	(Nothing moves. Then JACK COMPOSITE groans.)
JACK.	The atmosphere in here was unbearable till we moved Arthur down the corridor. Welcome Gordon. I'm Jack Composite. Elected shop steward for this secret caucus.
GORDON.	Time is short, comrade.
JACK.	Great to hear that word again. We couldn't bear the icy indifference.
CHARLIE.	Keep it low gents.
	(ENTER the GHOST of JOHN SMITH.)
JOHN SMITH'S GHOST.	Remember. I was most foully murdered.
JACK.	Course I remember.
GHOST.	I'm glad you do. You're next on the list. Tell him, Gordon.
GORDON.	Tony-Boy's planning to merge the TUC with the CBI. They've even got the acronym ready for national launch. TWISTBASE: Third Way Institute Of Social Tactics For Business And Customer Executives.
JACK.	We're not customers. I'm not an executive. On the train I'm a passenger. In life I'm a worker and a trades unionist. I'm not a bleeding colleague. I'm a comrade.
CHARLIE.	Keep it down, colleague.
JACK.	Who is this geezer-bird?

CHARLIE.	Shut yer gob. We're here to help you. (Aside.) I used to be a trade unionist myself. 'Til the Thatcher pump was put on me.
JACK.	She put it on all of us. It's bled everything away. And still no drinks at number ten. Do something, Gordon.
GORDON.	Drinks at number eleven next week.
JACK.	They blamed us for the downturn in the seventies. But can they blame us now? The tidal wave from the Far East, drowning Newcastle factories? Do you know what's really going on in the world?
GHOST.	I do.
JACK.	But you're not here. We've got to wake up, before everything is mangled. We don't even know the words for things anymore.
GHOST.	I do.
CHARLIE.	The dead are so boring, because they're always right.
GHOST.	Hattersley isn't.
GORDON.	Listen, Jack. One day, soon, Tony-Boy will go just one step too far. Then we will need to act. Swiftly, smoothly, brutally. I'll push my furniture straight through his walls.
GHOST.	Remember, where power goes, wealth flows.
GORDON.	Tony-Boy says where wealth lies only there will power rise.

(The GHOST makes to EXIT.)

JACK.	He's not one of us. He's in the pocket of the greedy bastards,

	vomiting over the trough. Are you going to do anything about that? I've seen leaders come and go. Why are you any different?
GORDON.	I'm all you've got. Tell them, old mole in socialism's cellar, what kind of leader will I be?
GHOST.	You have two choices. Frank Sinatra. Loved by all those who did not know him. Hated by those who did and . . .
GORDON.	What's the other choice?
GHOST.	Over a thousand years ago in ancient China the scholar Lao-Tzu spoke these words of wisdom: 'A leader is best When people barely know he exists Not so good when people obey and acclaim him Worse when they despise him But of a good leader, who talks little, When his work is done, his aim fulfilled, They will say: We did it ourselves.'
JACK.	Do something.
GHOST.	(Doom voice.) Do something.
JACK.	Do something before he melts us down.
GORDON.	What can you deliver? Have you any battalions left?
JACK.	Millions part-time. Millions casual. Millions disappeared. Walked out of the system. Can't call them out.
GHOST.	Do something.

CHARLIE.	Let's get out of here Gordon. Political necrophilia can be infectious.
GHOST & JACK.	Do something.
GORDON.	This is the nightmare of modern politics. We live in times where politicians can do nothing. It's not easy to plough the sea.
GHOST.	Politicians who believe that will become nothing. Stir yourself Gordon. Scotland beckons.

SCENE TWELVE

LORD CHANCELLOR'S OFFICE

Images of Henry VIIIth on wall-paper. The CARDINAL is pacing back and forth.

CARDINAL.	Sit on Woolsack. Stand up from Woolsack. Take one pace left. Ask: My Lords who is content among you? As one of Lords says 'Content.' One pace to right. Sit down on Woolsack. Stand up from Woolsack. Oh damn, I must get this right. That young woman with a scrawny bum from the newspapers, said I have a pathological fear of making a fool of myself. Rubbish. Utter rubbish. I do have a pathological fear of scrawny bums. Of course the great Cardinal wore a hair-shirt. He was never as fat as Orson Welles. Bloody Hollywood. Shakespeare's Cardinal was the most cultured and the most politically sophisticated man in the

kingdom. I could have played him. I am playing him.

(Enter TONY-BOY.)

My Sovereign, I confess your royal graces
Showered on me daily have been more than could
My studied purposes requite, which went
Beyond all man's endeavours . . .

TONY-BOY.	Please don't Dub-Dub. Ugly rumours.
CARDINAL.	I've heard. Madame Tussaud's. Bad, bad. The Leader of the Opposition meeting the TUC in secret.
TONY-BOY.	Dub-Dub. As Lord Chancellor enlighten me. Does the unwritten constitution specify that the Chancellor of the Exchequer is always the Leader of the Opposition?
CARDINAL.	No, no. New tradition. Only started when Michael Foot became Leader of the Labour Party. Are you worried?
TONY-BOY.	Not really, really. (A PAUSE.) Should I be?
CARDINAL.	What do you think?
TONY-BOY.	I'm asking you.
CARDINAL.	Sack Gordon.
TONY-BOY.	It would split the party.
CARDINAL.	Wrong. This party is as flexible and flaccid as the President's penis on its round of interns. But it has a bloom now. It is malleable. Shapeless plasticine in your hands.

TONY-BOY.   (A PAUSE.) And mine.
                 I think, for once, I'm not going to
                 accept your advice Dub-Dub. You
                 see, when the money goes funny
                 and it usually does. Even under
                 Margaret money went funny. Then I
                 will need a scapegoat.

CARDINAL.   It is a privilege, my prince, to
                 observe the pupil outshine his
                 master. Occasionally.

TONY-BOY.   Oh goodness, well what can I say.

CARDINAL.   A glass of claret might help.

TONY-BOY.   Should I Summit Gordon at number
                 ten? Try and be friends again?

CARDINAL.   (Ignoring that.) Do you think I'm
                 an arrogant bully?

TONY-BOY.   Since this is a day for honesty, I'll
                 tell you. No. (A PAUSE.) And I
                 don't really mean yes.

CARDINAL.   Meet him alone. He is a man who is
                 insecure, but pretends he is tough.
                 He wants to be loved, but never can
                 be. He tells us he is efficient but his
                 sock drawer is in permanent chaos,
                 like the economy. He acts as if he
                 were gregarious but prefers his own
                 company. He loves long
                 engagements but no longer can
                 resist the photo opportunity offered
                 by the altar. Play on his neuroses,
                 massage his melancholy, young
                 Tony-Boy. (A PAUSE.) Now for
                 important matters of state. You
                 know I've always felt Hampton
                 Court is under-used. Small rooms
                 permanently eavesdropping on big
                 rooms. Candlelight dinners. Perfect
                 Tudor system of sewage disposal.

	Could I move my offices there, Tony-Boy?
TONY-BOY.	How would you commute?
CARDINAL.	It's only five minutes by helicopter.

SCENE THIRTEEN

SUMMIT POLITICS – A COLD WAR BETWEEN WARM FRIENDS

POLLY on her mobile.

POLLY.	Do you hear me? This is a private meeting. I want the room unbugged. What do you mean you can't? Put me on to Stella. Stella, be a juicy little peach, I want our meeting room unbugged. You better do it. As you know Gordon's questioning your budget allocation. Thank you very much. (Aside.) Details, details.

No. 10. A meeting room. TONY-BOY and CHARLIE are facing each other, arms out. They are being frisked, TONY-BOY by CHARLIE and GORDON by POLLY. The spin doctors remove revolvers, microphones, hammers, icepicks etc. From their clothes.

POLLY.	He's clean.
CHARLIE.	He's clean.
	(EXIT all but TONY-BOY and GORDON. POLLY eavesdrops. TONY-BOY and Gordon move to centre-stage and give each other an Italian hug.)
TONY-BOY.	Colleague.
GORDON.	Colleague. Thanks for the ginseng tablets. Much appreciated.

TONY-BOY.	Thank you for the guarana. Cherry-Pop said I was a new man.
	(A horrible silence.)
GORDON.	Should we unspin?
TONY-BOY.	If you really, really want.
POLLY.	(Aside.) This is dangerous. An unspun conversation.
CHARLIE.	(Aside.) This is bad. An unspun conversation.
TONY-BOY.	Leave us alone.
	(EXIT all except TONY-BOY and GORDON.)
TONY-BOY.	What happened to us, Gordon? We used to share a dream.
POLLY.	(Aside.) Have you noticed the amazing dexterity With which he oozes such petit-bourgois sincerity? Soon you'll see the tears in his eyes Usually saved for when Royalty dies.
TONY-BOY.	(a LITTLE TEAR.) You remember how your parents, like mine, used to say to us: just do your best, boys.
GORDON.	What's wrong with you? You're beginning to speak like those kids who write your speeches.
TONY-BOY.	I've not changed. You have. What's made you so bitter, Gordon? We used to eat together, laugh together, shit on the same people together. I mean I even let you play with my guitar. You've become embittered and twisted, Gordon.
GORDON.	Let's be straight with each other. The deal was you become leader

	and we share not a dream, but power. Just like Hillary and Bill, Little and Large, Vic and Bob, Beavis and Butt Head. Instead you share power like Stalin and Trotsky.
TONY-BOY.	We don't want history. History is so destructive. It makes things so bitter.
GORDON.	Does it so.
TONY-BOY.	We all have to grow-up, Gordon. And you're still playing games. I know what happened in the trades-union room at the waxworks.
GORDON.	Just making sure we don't lose touch with our supporters.
	(TONY-BOY blinks. Then shakes his head.)
TONY-BOY.	The old divisive passions that destroyed Great Britain and created a feel-bad situation. Forget the old emotions. People are so much happier without them.
GORDON.	I'll argue this in Cabinet.
TONY-BOY.	I'm thinking that the Cabinet shouldn't meet at all. We can send round options. Then ministers can reply by punching buttons on their telephones. The way we vote in the party. Think new. Become new. That's our Formula One. The country needs re-branding. Think Virginal. Digital. Heathrow IS the world's busiest airport. We need terminals in every home. We are the land of Sir Walter Scott, Sir Walter Raleigh, Captain Cook, Princess Di, Lord Sainsbury, and Biggles. Biggles reminds me of Ivanhoe.

POLLY.	(Aside.) Given the dumbed-down state which we are creating, I think it might help if I told you who all these people are. Sir Walter Scott was a Scottish novelist who wrote a book called Ivanhoe which won the Booker prize. Sir Walter Raleigh invented the bicycle. Captain Cook was an eighteenth-century travel agent. Princess Di was a much-loved working class florist in Kensington. Lord Sainsbury is the Jehovah of our new democracy, a chicken in every mushroom pie. Biggles you will meet. Savour the surprise.
TONY-BOY.	Biggles reminds me of Ivanhoe.
GORDON.	You once called me Ivanhoe.
TONY-BOY.	But that was a long time ago and in another country. You're caught in history's offside trap. I do worry about you. Why hasn't our elixir worked on you? Is there something in the Scottish gene that resists change?
GORDON.	We modernised together.
TONY-BOY.	What you thought we were modernising I was destroying. I'm fed-up with fights between carrots and radishes. I mean, why should aubergines and courgettes be seen as rivals? There's been too much discord in our land. Now we must agree.
GORDON.	About what?
TONY-BOY.	That we agree. Let's agree to agree. Polly and Charlie will spin that we do anyway. I love agreements. That moment when you walk out of the

	door to the microphone and just say: 'We agree.'
GORDON.	But what about politics? Diversity? Issues? Getting our own back? Reality has become petrified for you.
TONY-BOY.	Let's just agree, Gordon. The future could be very beautiful.
GORDON.	'A nation not slow or dull, but of quick, ingenious and piercing spirit, acute to invent, subtle and sinewy to discourse, not beneath the reach of any point that human capacity can soar to.'
TONY-BOY.	Gosh. Did Charlie write that for you?
GORDON.	He pinched it from Milton. Who wrote it for Cromwell.
TONY-BOY.	Gosh yes. Milton spun well. I think I might use it.
GORDON.	You can't, it's mine you bastard.
POLLY.	(Aside.) Milton was a famous blind jazz pianist and songwriter. Cromwell was a moderniser who built a road in London that still bears his name.
GORDON.	Don't get carried away, Tony-Boy. Any moment you'll trip someone up in the box. And as night follows day, the penalty will come. Politics will out. What then?
TONY-BOY.	Go home, kind Cassius, Go home.
	(He EXITS.)
POLLY.	(Aside. Squawk-like.) We'll never fall from power. Ever. Never. We'll be the longest lasting Government

                        in British history.

                        (She EXITS.)

GORDON.   Why oh why did I ever let this guy
                        take the party? How did we plant
                        this alien bush in England's fair
                        garden? Its poisoned roots choking
                        all that grows around it, destroying
                        the soil in which our institutions
                        grow? Bring out the secateurs,
                        Gordon, prune, cut, dig out the roots.
                        Purify the soil and replant . . . ME.
                        Or am I doomed to be a weeping
                        willow tree? No, not that. I am
                        beginning to feel heated and
                        animated. To Idaho I shall go to sup
                        with the Media-Baron. (He clutches
                        his head.) A long spoon, a long
                        spoon, my kingdom for a long
                        spoon.

                        (He EXITS.)

SCENE FOURTEEN

THE POWER OF THE UNDEAD

Darkened, gloomy Downing Street. CHERRY-POP with
divining rod.

CHERRY-POP.   Down through Downing Street at
                        night. Past all the dead Prime
                        Ministers on the wall. To a living
                        dead Prime Minister in the
                        basement. Sh sh, beware security.

                        (In the basement THATCHER is
                        pouring an entire bottle of whisky
                        into a bowl. She stirs, witch-like.)

THATCHER.   I know that look. It reminds me of
                        Denis.

CHERRY-POP. Yes. Living with power. How did Denis manage?

THATCHER. He played the fool. (She points into the bowl.) That kept him in good spirits.

CHERRY-POP. My yogi won't let me drink.

THATCHER. Yogis are taking over British culture, they should all be deported. You need new guidelines. Stay out of the world of power, dear. Reclaim your own life.

CHERRY-POP. I try to. I defend all the serial killers I can. But the world of politics always intrudes.

THATCHER. (Stirring the liquid in the bowl.) Live your own life, you sad little woman. Politicians give up real life. We have to live in a world cocooned from reality. Otherwise we can't make the right decisions. This becomes even more important in the digital age.

CHEERY-POP. You sound like Tony-Boy.

THATCHER. I think the word you're looking for is symbiosis.

(POLLY appears.)

POLLY. Symbiosis. It's when you mix carrot juice and tomato juice and they begin to taste the same.

THATCHER. I'm very pleased with Tony-Boy you know, but he must go all the way.

CHERRY-POP. All the way to where?

THATCHER. I'm talking history dear, not the Wizard of Oz. (A PAUSE.) To make an impact a modern Prime Minister must destroy a Union.

CHERRY-POP.	He's thinking about the teachers . . .
THATCHER.	No no, the tougher choice is nurses. We found we didn't need train guards or bus conductors. We can do just as well without nurses. Let unemployed relatives and old-age pensioners come in and clean up the mess.
CHERRY-POP.	You haven't lost your style. Tell me Margaret, have you any regrets?
THATCHER.	My only regret is that Tony-Boy was never in my cabinet. He would have been so . . . What do they say? . . . interactive. Now run along dear and keep him strong.

SCENE FIFTEEN

**PILLOW POLICY –
A SCENE FROM A MODERN MARRIAGE**

TONY-BOY is preparing for bed. THATCHER and CHERRY-POP cross the stage, THATCHER with a large bottle of whisky as they do so.

THATCHER.	Sh! Sh! Sh!
POLLY.	(Aside. Hissing.) I hate old style nuclear family relationships. Wife comes on. Powerful man explains his dilemmas to wife as they retire for the day.
CHERRY-POP.	(Aside.) Wife comes on. Spin doctor goes off. (EXIT POLLY, cross.) Darling, what are the guidelines of our relationship?
TONY-BOY.	Quick wins?

CHERRY-POP.	Quick wins. Yes, that is our style.
TONY-BOY.	It is, really. Yes, it is.
CHERRY-POP.	Lots of quick wins. Like . . . privatise sections of the Army on the purchaser-provided principle.
TONY-BOY.	Think the unthinkable? What about giving allotments to single mums and work-shy boys?
CHERRY-POP.	It could be argued that all we were doing was encouraging them to grow organic vegetables. Sell them in street markets. We monitor the sales and subtract the profits from their handouts. It could save us a lot of money and do everyone some good. Self-reliance.
TONY-BOY.	Schools.
CHERRY-POP.	Teachers' Unions.
TONY-BOY.	They are the enemy within.
CHERRY-POP.	De-unionise the schools.
TONY-BOY.	Let the Media-Baron run the schools on his satellites. He makes a lot of money and we set free education. You are wonderful, a trained mind. Think unthinkable about Gordon.
CHERRY-POP.	Quick-win unthinkable? Simple. Make Robin Cook the Chancellor. He'll be a terrible leader of the opposition.
TONY-BOY.	(Smiling.) I know. He's such a disappointment. Why were we all so scared of him? (They kiss.) I can't. Better to have Gordon sulking next door than setting up his tent at Stirling Castle.

CHERRY-POP.	(Telephone rings. A strange light begins to flash.) Oh dear, it's the emergency hot rod from Washington.
	(A telephone is lowered. TONY-BOY takes hold of it.)
TONY-BOY.	Mr President? Of course I'm wide awake. Just watching the sun set on the River Thames.
	(CHERRY-POP giggles.)
	Oh I know. The Bonfire Of Liberties Bill went through. Only twenty voted against. They can see their solicitors in seven days. What . . . what Bill? New airstrikes, excellent. These bombs strengthen democracy everywhere. I'll inform the Defence and Foreign Secretaries in the morning. Do you mind telling where the eh . . . targets are? (Sits bolt upright.) Could I negotiate a twenty-four hour delay? I'm very good at negotiating. I might persuade them to surrender. Twelve hours. Thank you so much Mr President, most grateful. (Telephone flies away. He turns in horror to CHERRY-POP.) He says we have Islamics here. He wants to bomb Bradford, Birmingham and the mosque in Regent's Park. He says they have the exact location of terrorists cells. He says there won't be any collateral damage. I hope his intelligence is as good as it was in the Sudan.
CHERRY-POP.	Relax, my very own little Emperor. Never mind America, Europe is

	going our way. Who needs a Grand Army when you've got style? (A PAUSE.) Should we try the third way tonight?
TONY-BOY.	Must we? It hurts my knees so. Just sing me to sleep, M'lud.
	(As Tony-Boy smiles beatifically as she sings her lullaby.)
CHERRY-POP'S LULLABY.	
	Sleep, Tony, Sleep Deep may you slumber No ideas your thoughts encumber Shares they are rising Polls climbing too Focus groups are all in bed Thinking of you. Few think you're nasty. Few think you're mean. Dream on Napoleon I'm your Josephine.
POLLY.	(Aside.) Ahhh. (Sick.) Urrrgh. You'll all need a drink after that. So off you all go to the lovely Tricycle bar. As you are going out please do not look directly into the security camera because of retinal damage.

(INTERVAL.)

SCENE SIXTEEN
CHARLIE FARRAGO – SOUTH LONDON'S VERY OWN

Great to hear some of you mouth off in the bar about Tony-Boy. 'Specially as all my money's on Gordon.

(She sings.)

Gordon Gordon what do I have to do
I'm half crazy spinning away for you –
I'd love to be running the story
Of your secret backstabbing for glory
'Cos you'd look neat
In the leader's seat
Of a party not made for two.

Enough of singsongs, screaming wheels time. The scene shifts to Idaho in the U.S. of A and so do I.

(She EXITS.)

SCENE SEVENTEEN
WHERE HAVE ALL THE PRINCIPLE'S GONE? GONE TO IDAHO, EVERY ONE

MEDIA-BARON's office. A screen, desk. The MEDIA-BARON is alone à la Citizen Kane. He's looking at the screen.

(Melancholy.) Round and round the world I go, day and night decisions.

(Perks up.) OK. British Government time. If I'm going to dump Tony-Boy, let's parade the runners.

(MARGARET BECKETT appears. A SILENCE.)

Next up.

(DAVID BLUNKETT appears.)

Didn't like 'Shopping And Fucking.' A Minister of Education incapable of understanding the basic dialectical structure of post-modern theatre. The man is a national disgrace. Next up.

(ROBIN COOK on screen.)

If I'd wanted ethics I'd have hired Spinoza.

(JACK STRAW on screen.)

A liberal in jackboots. I like it. But the Nixon problem. Looks shifty after five o'clock. Send in the money man.

DISEMBODIED VOICE.

The Chancellor of the Exchequer of England is in reception.

MEDIA-BARON.

Put him in the holding suite and turn the muzak up. (To audience.) The responsibility weighs heavily on me. It's 3 am and I'm stuck here making and breaking politicians all over the world. You start with 'spot the ball' in the Billabong Gazette and fifty years later you're rearranging the orbit of the planet. Someone's got to do it.

(Enter GORDON.)

GORDON.	I'm nervous and edgy and trying to be suave. I fear ambition is over-riding my judgement. It's a private complaint I've suffered from before.
MEDIA-BARON.	You've come to the right doctor.
CHARLIE.	(Aside.) This isn't taking place.
GORDON.	Thanks very much for seeing me. This a delicate matter.
MEDIA-BARON.	Yeah. If Tony-Boy were to drop under a Eurostar, or try and fly from the Eiffel Tower or get seriously impaled on a Brandenburg Gate, the job's yours. My readers. Your focus-groups. England. The great steaming turkey squat upon the plate. (Charm.) What can I do for you? You're safe here. No MI6.
GORDON.	Would you want me to reverse my policies and go back on Europe?
MEDIA-BARON.	It's a man's world.
	(A PAUSE.)
	The sinews of Europe are coated with inscrutable malice.
GORDON.	I've never looked at it like that before.
MEDIA-BARON.	They hate my sort in Paris, Rome, Berlin. I was telling Berlosconi the other day that in years to come they would look back on me as the Leonardo Da Vinci of the 20th Century. He laughed.
GORDON.	Did he really. Well. But can I ask you again, do we have to dump the Euro to get your support?
	(A Long SILENCE.)
MEDIA-BARON.	You're now thinking of the art of the possible.

	(GORDON continues to think.) You're now thinking your party has always argued that without power it can achieve nothing.
	(GORDON thinks on.) You're now thinking Chequers. The swimming pool in the grounds. Built as a gift from Nixon: every time you take a dip you come out dirtier. But the view's wonderful. You are thinking . . .
GORDON.	Yes, yes, I am . . .
MEDIA-BARON.	Think on Macduff. You have a few months yet. But remember always seek the truth, it has no confines.
GORDON.	I have always believed we would only go in if conditions were right.
MEDIA-BARON.	But all my editors tell me conditions will never be right. It's an arithmetic of depression and despair. And I can tell you boy, a recession's on the way.
GORDON.	But then the pound will be weak, the labour market will be cowed and conditions for our entry will be perfect.
MEDIA-BARON.	What we think to be true isn't always the case.
GORDON.	Oh my god, Wittgenstein.
MEDIA-BARON.	Of what we cannot speak we must pass over in silence
GORDON.	A last gesture of goodwill. If I become Prime Minister, it would be a honour to have you in my Cabinet.
MEDIA-BARON.	But I'm not in your party. I'm not an MP. I'm not even British.

GORDON.	That doesn't matter anymore. in forty-eight hours you'll be in the House of Lords. It's your experience we're after. It's your business sweep. You are the only man who can run businesses world-wide probably without any money at all. Britain needs your experience.
MEDIA-BARON.	I'm already running seven Governments. I just want to use your island as a base to buy Europe.
GORDON.	Yes. Well. Good. We'll meet again soon.
	(GORDON leaves the presence. He hastens to CHARLIE.)
	What d'you think?
CHARLIE.	It went well. But while we've been here the enemy's set something up.
GORDON.	What? What?
CHARLIE.	An intimate rooftop party for businessmen on the top of the D.T.I. They're given some kind of Award. It's a Nobel Prize for profits. You know? (Sinisterly.) A cheque the size of the London Underground?
GORDON.	Money can't buy you love. Let's get home.
	(They EXIT.)

SCENE EIGHTEEN

A PERSONALITY PROBLEM

TONY-BOY and POLLY alone.

TONY-BOY.	I can't stand Biggles. He's like a whale's blubber.

POLLY.	Spin that for me Tony-Boy.
TONY-BOY.	I'm speaking metaphorically. There's so much fat between us and what's really inside him.
POLLY.	But he's on a permanent diet of caviar and organic hair dye.
TONY.	It's a spiritual thing.
POLLY.	Oh.
TONY.	He's too alternative for my taste. He's not one of us. Why does he object to wearing clothes?
POLLY.	He is the most popular, monied type of person in the land. He is the people's business man. That's why he must be made one of us. Clear?

SCENE NINETEEN

BUTTERING UP TO BIGGLES – BUT JUST HOW BIG IS HIS BIGNESS?

POLLY.	(Aside.) Beautiful morning. Sunshine. Can you hear the twitter of cameramen above the birds? Go birds, go cameramen. This is what I love. The flow of photo opportunities.
	(ENTER CHERRY-POP.)
	Oh Cherry-Pop, don't get photo'ed with an exit sign over your head.
CHEERY-POP.	There's an unstable energy field here harmful to us.
POLLY.	That's just the euro on the Frankfurt Stock Exchange. We're bound to feel it here.

	(ENTER BIGGLES. In public he is charming and sunny and straightforward. In private he is grumpy, cussed and humourless.)
BIGGLES.	(Shaking hands.) Prime Minister, Mrs Cherry-Pop, Secretary of State. (Give POLLY a polite kiss.) Thank you so much for inviting me to give the DTI Business Man of the Decade Award.
TONY-BOY.	Delighted your diary was free.
BIGGLES.	But why am I really here?
TONY-BOY.	So that we could really get to know each other.
BIGGLES.	Why?
TONY-BOY.	Because your country needs you.
BIGGLES.	Why?
TONY-BOY.	(Becoming desperate.) Shall we discuss this after the ceremony?
BIGGLES.	(Dully.) Oh yah. Sociable mode. (He is at once bright, likeable and breezy.) I'm dying to know who's got it. Right, I must do my speech now. I hope you like it. Sir Malvolio Clapper's made me sweat blood on this one.
	(Behind, to loud applause, a balloon basket is revealed. Its ropes disappear aloft, but the basket is earthbound. Speeches are into bright, loud-sounding microphones. BIGGLES leaps up on the balloon. In contrast to his private manner, his speech is manic.)
BIGGLES.	Hello. Welcome. Au revoir. Bonjour. Ola! Gotterdammerung mein pickled herren. Before I give

the Award, a word about Heaven. What we're trying to do at Heaven airlines, Heaven cola, Heaven zoos, Heaven Mercenaries Inc., Heaven record stores, Heaven designer rags and our much hated Heaven trains, is to move on. We are always moving on. We are sending me to be the first person to reach the North Pole on a Heaven skateboard. After this ceremony we will be flying to Morocco to retrieve our Heaven skateboard from the Moroccan authorities. 1.4 people live in countries where English has official status. We are always trying to learn from that. Now it is my privilege to present the Award.

(POLLY hands him a large gold envelope.)

And the winner of the DTI Business Man of the Century is . . .
(A PAUSE.) Me. And the prize money is in Euros. I'm dumb with modesty. Prime Minister?

(A football chant of 'Are you watching, Are you watching, are you watching Singapore?')

TONY-BOY.   Gosh. Well. So many Euro friends. What can I say? You know it is very important. And, dear Biggles, I would like to say this in public. Biggles knows that life is a Lottery. And if you don't get a lot of Lottery the first time, you just wait. In the end as Biggles has taught us, talent wins.

(Applause and a football chant of 'are you watching Singapore?')

TONY-BOY.	(Now in private.) Look Biggles I mean to say, I really really meant to say for a long time, would you really like to buy the London Underground?
BIGGLES.	Why? (A PAUSE.) How much?
TONY-BOY.	We'll give you a subsidy of one billion pounds. Surely that's enough to do it up and sell it on.
BIGGLES.	Heaven Heavenly underground. Underground Heaven. Always check the logo. The deed might be done.
CHERRY-POP.	(Taking BIGGLES aside.) Tony-Boy really would like you to elect you as our new Dick Whittington.
BIGGLES.	Why?
CHERRY-POP.	Because of your charm.
BIGGLES.	Go charm now? (He is his public, bright persona.) I am a political virgin. I'm not a member of any party.
CHERRY-POP.	That doesn't matter, we all go to the same parties.
TONY-BOY.	People love leaders who can rise above parties.
BIGGLES.	Logo check. Would virginal politics make a Heavenly mayor?
CHERRY-POP.	You magnificent hunk with your big balloon.
BIGGLES.	Logos always work.
TONY-BOY.	People trust you because you take risks. When at anytime your balloon bursts and you fall, for example, on the very sharp minarets of Teheran, when we've flown your body back

	there will be more people at your funeral than at Hers . . .
BIGGLES.	Are you sure?
CHERRY-POP.	We're sure.
TONY-BOY.	You are the people's business man.
BIGGLES.	I'm not quite certain whether you want me to be Mayor of London before or after I'm dead.
TONY-BOY.	Whichever you prefer. Polly can swing it either way.
BIGGLES.	I'll reflect on it the next time I'm hanging over the Sahara.
POLLY.	(Aside.) The Sahara is not a dry martini cocktail at the American Bar at the Savoy, it is a fourwheel drive off-roader vehicle. Boss, time for approach mode.
TONY-BOY.	Biggles, may I – privately – swing open a window of policy opportunity?
BIGGLES.	(Sudden flash of the public manner. A big smile.) Yeah, sure, privileged.
TONY-BOY.	You see . . . You know what we've done, why we've done it, and what we've learnt. But you don't know what we intended to do next. You see, the people have lost faith in all our institutions, and I fear they may be right. I mean, our institutions are really quite awful.
BIGGLES.	The only institution I've ever believed in is my bank. (Bright persona.) You may be on the right track. We might, not will, and maybe not, do business together. A billion and a half.

POLLY.   (Aside.) Insider information, a
                          criminal act can work like can
                          aphrodisiac. (With a sigh.) It's the
                          sexiest thing.

                          (They are all EXITING as
                          GORDON ENTERS.)

                          (To GORDON.) Late again.

GORDON.   Is your party finished?

POLLY.   We're moving on.

                          (GORDON EXITS the other way in
                          a huff.)

SCENE TWENTY

SIX QUESTIONS ON POWER

CARDINAL's chambers. For once he is buried deep in legal papers. CHERRY-POP comes on dressed as a lawyer. They pinch each other's bums as if it were a Masonic ritual.

CARDINAL.   To what do I owe this fragrant
                          pleasure in my workspace?

CHERRY-POP.   The rod of power guided me to
                          your chambers. It's so reassuring to
                          know you're always at your post,
                          tied to it like a martyr.

CARDINAL.   Someone's got to keep the ship
                          afloat.

CHERRY-POP.   Dub-Dub I'm really worried. Can a
                          humble subordinate asked a great
                          lawyer six questions?

CARDINAL.   Always a delight to be cross-
                          examined by the face that launched
                          a thousand careers, including mine.
                          Turn the screws. Tie me in knots.

CHERRY-POP.   Then I put it to you. Do you think
                          all is well with the Government?

CARDINAL. There's nothing wrong with the Government that can't be cured by what's right with the Government.

CHERRY-POP. Is there such a thing as a value judgement? Should one ever turn down a client?

CARDINAL. Should a politician ever turn down a vote?

CHERRY-POP. Why aren't we worried about interfering with newspapers, the BBC, the orchestras, telling people what music they should like, putting nasty stories in the papers about radio editors we don't like? Will we get away with it till the election?

CARDINAL. Let me explain the constitutional position. The Government governs the country. The Government is, de facto, the country. It is impossible, de jure, to interfere with itself. The advantage of an unwritten constitution is that it can always make unconstitutional measures, legal.

CHERRY-POP. I speak for people everywhere. How does one deal with noisy neighbours? Doesn't Gordon worry you too?

CARDINAL. Ambition can never counteract ambition.

CHERRY-POP. Two Chief Constables told me that if we legalised cannabis, the crime statistics would fall, after all, Dub-Dub . . .

CARDINAL. The Drugs Czar is sound. (Freaking out.) Cannabis rots the brain. The appetite is lost. Stomach. Intestines become dysfunctional. Gall bladder

	inflamed. Eyes become a bilious yellow. Sex organs adversely affected. Good character traits disappear. Bad ones take over. (A PAUSE.) My wine merchant would never speak to me again.
CHERRY-POP.	Finally let me put it to you, that power corrupts everyone regardless of narrow party interest. Reassure me, Dub-Dub. It's not happening to Tony-Boy, is it?
CARDINAL.	Power is like fire. If you watch gently, it warms, if you provoke it too much it scorches. But, if you increase it without control, it might destroy you. In this Government I am the control. Look at these fingers.
	(She backs away.)

SCENE TWENTY-ONE

DOME PARTY.

A Dome Cool Britannia Party. Flashing lights. Media celebs – dummies. TONY-BOY and POLLY. Banner: Show Business is Big Business.

TONY.	(With a cordless mike in his hand.) Gosh well, everyone's here. We've healed the old wounds now, we can all be together again. You know, people say we are dumbing down, but we're not. It's the third way. People love the quizzes on Radio Four. Why shouldn't the Today Programme discuss mushy peas in the House of Commons canteen? This is what a learning society is all about. We don't want issue-based

politics, we want knowledge based politics. We have ended the era of endings and begun the era of beginnings. I mean, if you don't like something, like thick-cut marmalade, or a play by Sir David Hare, they accuse you of dumbing down. Let's hang out with this. I mean, the apostles were accused of dumbing down Jesus.

(TONY-BOY continues to speak in mime. CHARLIE and GORDON ENTER, hanging about at the back of the crowd.)

GORDON. I can't take the Tony-Speak anymore.

CHARLIE. Feel the chill? Walkies?

GORDON. Yes, I think time to slink from the King's tent.

(They slip away.)

CHARLIE. You say the same but only in more difficult language. Remember when you were talking about something applying to 'freely reproducible commodities, those not subject to a natural resource, or other input?' And remember when you introduced us to the notion 'of a privileged endogenous determinant.' And remember when . . .

GORDON. Clear as a bell, what's the matter with you?

(They walk on.)

CHARLIE. Look, my Lord, it comes.

(ENTER the GHOST.)

GHOST. Why, why do you not remember?

	Why consort with the Media-Baron? He will most foully murder you.
GORDON.	Age has mellowed him. I found the hair peeping out from beneath his cuffs strangely attractive.
GHOST.	Have you lost your reason? Are you sinking into madness? Outside the battlements of Europe there is no future.
GORDON.	But the Media-Baron says something is rotten at the heart of Europe, Ghost.
GHOST.	Beware the capricious demons of the self-made rich. Listen, oh listen, Gordy-Boy, if you ever did your dead leader love.
GORDON.	O God!
GHOST.	Speed now. Speed to France and embrace your brother Jospin. Inform him of our murder and seek his help to raise by social contract such a force of arms that will win you the throne. Remember.

(Back to Dome Party.)

TONY-BOY.	We need a social-investment state. We need investment in human capital. Did you get that?
CHARLIE.	Is this the spinner's dream? Are we going for it? The Full Monty? Power? Bloodletting? Coup? Yes? Oh let's, let's, please? Should I ring Paxman at home?
GORDON.	I forbid you to reveal the secrets of my tortured soul. For the moment.

(EXIT.)

SCENE TWENTY-TWO
FRENCH LESSONS

CHARLIE. (Aside.) And so our scene to France must fly. For a little touch of Jospin in the night. To strengthen our sinews and prepare the fight.

France comes on. PRIME MINISTER JOSPIN is dressed in football gear and rasta wig, trying to look black. ENTER GORDON.

GORDON. I came to see Monsieur Jospin.

JOSPIN. I am Jospin. I am Chirac. I am France.

GORDON. I see. Well I'm really pleased you won the World Cup. (A PAUSE.) I've come for some help.

JOSPIN. It's too late. You could never have won. Because you belong to a dead country.

GORDON. I came to discuss politics, not football.

JOSPIN. Politics, football, Thatcherism wiped you out. Her Tony-fils is not much different. There is no Third way to win the World Cup and run an economy. You will never win the World Cup and run a proper economy. You will never win your stupid cup in Wimbledon. You want all your unemployed to be like ball boys, not players. You are bad even at a game you yourselves invented, crikett. You are so busy producing spin doctors, you have no spin bowlers. You have a problem, my friend. Your destiny is in the wrong hands.

GORDON.   (Flabbergasted.) But what if Scotland . . .

JOSPIN.   Ah. Ecosse. That could be different. There is a tradition of a collective passing game. They could be like us. Now go back to your stupid country and ask yourselves why it is the Eurostar is smooth and fast in France but slow and inefficient and wobbly in England. Perhaps your market is too flexi? Go and do not trouble me again. Unless . . .

GORDON.   (Eager.) Unless?

JOSPIN.   Forget middle England. Go to the Northern extremities of your islands, and lead your people somewhere.

GORDON.   Scotland? But my career . . .

JOSPIN.   In England you have no career. They will blame you for the recession. Ministers of Finance rise and fall with the stockmarket. You mean well, but farewell. I am the winning team. Vive la France, noir et blanc et bleu.

GORDON.   Go to Scotland? Do I have the character?

SCENE TWENTY-THREE

THE CRISIS COMETH

CARDINAL's chambers. TONY BOY, CARDINAL and POLLY. They are unrolling wallpaper. They are replacing the Henry VIII Holbein-style wallpaper with 'page 3' newspaper.

CARDINAL.   Does the Minister For Culture really want me to put this up?

TONY-BOY.   Yes. It's a gift from the Media-Baron.

CARDINAL.   (Mumbling.) In that case excellent. Bit weak on quality control.

                     (POLLY ENTERS in a rush.)

POLLY.   (To TONY.) Did you authorise Gordon's trip to Paris?

CARDINAL.   Junketing at the Ritz is he? The Aitken Suite. Ah. Sweet memory. (POLLY frowns.) A wine-tasting in Bordeaux. A fizzy little Chirac.

TONY-BOY.   That's my drink.

POLLY.   He's gone to taste the Chateau Jospin, I fear. A social communion wine.

CARDINAL.   Undrinkable.

TONY-BOY.   Is he on-message? Page him at once.

POLLY.   He and Charlie left their pagers in the VIP toilet at Heathrow. MI5 have just returned them to my office.

TONY-BOY.   Only yesterday Polly you told me he'd done a deal with the Media-Baron.

POLLY.   That too. He is beginning to disintegrate.

CARDINAL.   He's going Hattersley. Bad wine. Bad politics.

TONY-BOY.   I'm beginning to feel debriefed. Whenever Europe is mentioned I get this feeling ... that I've got no underpants on. Why does this happen to me, Cardinal?

CARDINAL.   I never wear underpants on principle. Makes life much easier.

TONY-BOY.   (Toying with his wallpaper brush.) How do we do this? We must be fair to Gordon. He has to go, but he must go fairly. Be seen to go fairly.

POLLY.   No third umpire. Clean bowled.

CARDINAL.   Henry's solution. The axe at Tower Hill.

POLLY.   But, as Margaret will advise you, no resignation speeches. I have a list here with one name. Someone who could replace him.

TONY-BOY.   (Taking the paper.) But Polly, it's your name on this paper.

                  (He throws the paper away without another thought.)

CARDINAL.   Why do we need a Chancellor of the Exchequer anyway? Let the fellow at the Bank of England run the money. The Prime Minister can do the budget. The whole bloody show's going to be run from Frankfurt anyway. All we're discussing is how we dress our window.

TONY-BOY.   Polly, we mustn't get isolated in our thinking. Focus-group us!

                  (A thunder-clap. The sofas with the focus-groups slam onto the stage tearing into wallpaper. A burst of the Archer's theme is heard.)

POLLY.   (To audience.) A little vote? Top up customer choice? Do we need a Chancellor Of The Excheqeur?

                  (The vote. Whatever it is POLLY says . . .)

POLLY.	Ninety-percent NO.
CARDINAL.	The price of democracy is a satellite dish, what? I'm in mentor mode. The High Lord Chancellor needs to be alone with his monarch.
POLLY.	I feel my presence is necessary, I do not wish you to contemplate the unspinnable.
CARDINAL.	Run along, dear. We'll send for you if you're needed.
	(All clear except Tony-Boy and Cardinal.)
POLLY.	(Aside.) We're all a bit paranoid these days. It's the zeitgeist. I know what they're going to say. The room's bugged.
	(POLLY EXITS.)
CARDINAL.	I'm sure this room is bugged. Let's speak in Latin. De Constitionus Brittanicus non existicus et est in non sequitor. Nihil Illegitimatum Carborundum.
POLLY.	(Aside.) MI5 computers are reading that as 'Don't let the bastards grind you down.' (Panics.) What is going on?
TONY-BOY.	Dub-Dub. The rose garden is the only safe place at No 10. I think. The roses are in full bloom.
	(Garden is wheeled on.)
POLLY.	(Desperate.) Charlie! Wherever you are. It's happening. I don't know what's happening. Control-freaks nightmare. Kiss. Make-up or we're dead. Are you listening Charlie?
CHARLIE.	(Disembodied voice.) Don't panic.

	We've bugged the roses.
TONY-BOY.	Is it really a crisis, Dub-Dub?
CARDINAL.	It's *the* crisis, Tony-Boy. If the Media-Baron turns the polls turn down, If you lose Gordon, you lose the Party.
TONY-BOY.	But I am the Party. I won power for them.
CARDINAL.	The price was too high. They hate you for it. Half your Cabinet are waiting for you to stumble. The other half are lobotomised. Time to clear the decks Tony-Boy.
TONY-BOY.	What do you mean, Dub-Dub? I'm lost. I'm in a dark wood. Certainties slink away from me. Think-tank me through this. Where is the Grail? What is the Grail?
CARDINAL.	The grail of modern politics is to create the illusion of change while making sure that nothing changes.
TONY-BOY.	We need to give the people what they think they really want.
CARDINAL.	Which is always the same as what we think they deserve. Make this the giving age.
TONY-BOY.	How do we do that?
CARDINAL.	As we have discussed many times, on Tuscan holidays, we need to do a really big change so things can never really change again.
TONY-BOY.	My very own Cardinal Wolsey.

SCENE TWENTY-FOUR

IN WHICH OUR SPINNERS EXPERIENCE A NASTY MOMENT

CHARLIE and POLLY on mobile phones. POLLY wander round stage and CHARLIE is somewhere in the theatre.

CHARLIE.	What's the Big Change?
POLLY.	Big what? Dunno.
CHARLIE.	Don't believe you.
POLLY.	I'm serious.
CHARLIE.	Are you out of orbit?
POLLY.	Sort of . . .
CHARLIE.	Oh my God! Tony-Boy's cutting you out, Polly. Squeezed like a black-head from the nose of the body-politic. Want to come over? Leg it round for me?
	(They meet. They look at each other.)
CHARLIE.	Friends?
POLLY.	We need to be if we're going to get back to a win-win situation.
CHARLIE.	Indicate Right and turn Left?
POLLY.	Indicate Left and Turn Right?
	(They hug and kiss.)
CHARLIE.	Ugh. Salt cod fish. Still eating Brazilian?
POLLY.	Friends!
CHARLIE.	Big Change. Big Change.
POLLY.	Big Change? Do you think he could sack me?
CHARLIE.	That's small change. Think big change. Think Big, Polly.

POLLY.	However hard I try I can't. My world is limited. Small envelopes of petty back-bites. Trivial leaks to TV channels. Rubbishing Gordon. Trying to get you sacked. Hiring and firing Editors at the Daily Express. You know it's rabid personal ambition that prohibits me from thinking about anything to do with real people. Even my strong sense of self-knowledge is no good at all.
CHARLIE.	When you go micro, macro is a nightmare. Find out what they're up to, Polly.
POLLY.	What happened in France? Did Gordon meet Jospin and the commies? Did the Media-Baron send you?
CHARLIE.	The Media-Baron? The world's a big place Polly. Europe is Media-Baronless.
POLLY.	That's the problem.
CHARLIE.	I get the impression you've been relocated. You don't know nothing.
POLLY.	You don't know nothing, not at all neither.
CHARLIE.	You don't know what I mean, you know what I mean?
POLLY.	Do.
CHARLIE.	Don't.
POLLY.	Do.
CHARLIE.	Don't.
POLLY.	(Startled.) Hang on. Dumb down for a minute. Is it my imagination? My phone hasn't rung for five minutes.

CHARLIE.	Oh my God. Nor has mine. Suddenly it feels as if all the mobile phone towers in the country have blown up. Are the lights going out all over Britannia?
	(Both their mobiles purr simultaneously.)
POLLY.	Thank God.
CHARLIE.	Thank God.
POLLY.	Yes Tony-Boy. There in a minute.
CHARLIE.	On my way Gordon.

SCENE TWENTY-FIVE

IN WHICH THE FINAL SUMMIT BETWEEN OUR HEROES IS BUGGED AND THE TRUTH IS SPUN

No 10. TONY-BOY and GORDON across a table. A chess time clock set is on the table. They speak and press. POLLY and CHARLIE in spinning positions facing audience.

TONY-BOY.	Nice time in France?
POLLY.	(Aside.) He means: screw you, I know what you're up to.
GORDON.	The roses are finished in Paris, but here they're in full bloom.
CHARLIE.	(Aside.) This is a reference to standard government listening devices being sold illegally by GCHQ to Jeffrey Archer to help him monitor the activities of one Kenneth Livingstone.
TONY-BOY.	Meeting with the Media-Baron. Went well?
POLLY.	(Aside.) Did he eat and inwardly digest you?

GORDON.	Tony-Boy, I really think we need a frank discussion.
CHARLIE.	(Aside.) I really am after your job.
TONY-BOY.	I agree, Gordon. I really, really do.
POLLY.	I know you're after my job.
TONY-BOY.	You know why we're fighting Gordon, the structures are wrong.
POLLY.	He's firing him. I do believe he's going to fire him.
GORDON.	I know a lot of people in the party who've thought that for a long time.
CHARLIE.	Dead bat. You can't fire me. The party loves me.
TONY-BOY.	No I mean the structures are tired. They aren't working for us. Real democracy needs to break out afresh.
POLLY.	(Puzzled.) Not firing him. Shuffling? Where to? Transport! That's it. Transport! Railtrack say a big crash is coming.
TONY-BOY.	There's too much adversarial politics around. Our voter-customers hate it on television. So much shouting that they keep watching that dog lying around, hoping he'll bite someone.
POLLY.	(Puzzled.) David Blunkett's dog more popular than parliament?
CHARLIE.	(Panic.) Can you have a dog as Chancellor of the Exchequer?
POLLY.	Nothing's impossible. Animal lobby's huge. Could neutralise the Countryside Campaign.

TONY-BOY. Don't you think we politicians are always getting in the way of real needs? Country before Party. Break with the narrowness of political life. Direct democracy. Without politics.

GORDON. I agree. Need a complete overhaul. Redesign the chamber. Cut out the fancy-dress. Change the electoral system to PR. Earls in furs, robes and buckled shoes. Out on the streets. Let them learn to deal with the kerb-crawlers. The Treasury will make some money available to subsidise their wigs on a non-hereditary basis after they've been income-assessed. Elected second chamber. No more need for Black Rod. I agree Tony-Boy. It's the only way. Enough of this medieval mummery.

CHARLIE. (A smile.) He means Abolish the Lord Chancellor.

GORDON. I do feel quite emotional about this.

CHARLIE. He's saying he still fancies him a bit.

TONY-BOY. I have no problems with emotions either. Mine is an emotional government. Princess Di's power was born out of emotions and there's nothing wrong with that. I'm a really, really, emotional person.

POLLY. He's saying he finds him physically repellent.

GORDON. Has the Policy Unit drafted the Bill?

TONY-BOY. (Worried.) What Bill?

GORDON. The real Constitutional Reform Bill that I have just outlined.

CHARLIE.	The shot across the bows.
TONY-BOY.	(Relieved.) The Cardinal is working on it.
POLLY.	The fuck off.
TONY-BOY.	Listen Gordon, there is a momentum for change. Will you move with it?
POLLY.	Those who are not for me are against our project.
GORDON.	Where? Where?
CHARLIE.	Lost on that one.
TONY-BOY.	I'm sorry.
GORDON.	Momentum moving to where?
CHARLIE.	Don't play tricks with me you arsehole.
TONY-BOY.	If you haven't understood where we are going by now you will never get there. And when I get there you won't recognise me or where we are.
POLLY.	Stop behaving like a quill on a fretful porcupine.
CHARLIE.	What? Double-spin?
	(Both spinners shrug their shoulders as if to say it's beyond them.)
GORDON.	Have you become a Buddhist Tony-Boy? Was it you who persuaded the Dalai Lama to advertise the BBC? I thought you were cuddling Cherry-Pop in the Catholic closet. The mystery of the world. Mysterious motives. Melancholy markets. The murky global sea. The flash of the fin of a Tiger shark.
CHARLIE.	Watch it Tony-Boy, events could bring you down.

TONY-BOY.	The time has come, something huge is approaching us, a refreshing powerful storm is brewing. Soon it will blow away all the laziness, indifference, prejudice against work and decaying boredom from our society.
CHARLIE.	Did you write that bit Polly?
POLLY.	Anton Chekhov, actually, a Russian playwright. Writes Yeltsin's speeches.
CHARLIE.	Must be that Mafia geezer we met at the Moscow Summit.
TONY-BOY.	You see what is approaching Britannia is a Big Change.
	(A silence. The spinners and GORDON are at a loss.)
POLLY.	(Aside.) Oh help me little baby Jesus. I've got to do something a spinner must never do. Ask him what he means.
POLLY/CHARLIE/GORDON.	(Together.) Big Change? What Big Change?
TONY-BOY.	We must give the people what they want. A new partnership for power.
	(TONY-BOY and POLLY EXIT. ENTER the GHOST of JOHN SMITH.)
GHOST.	Do not be deceived.
GORDON.	I know not what is this thing I have yet to do.
GHOST.	Remember. The Party.
GORDON.	What is Tony-Boy doing? What is his scenario? I am on-message but in heaven's name what is the message? What is Big Change?

GHOST.   Now Gordon, listen. While sleeping in the early Nineties a serpent stung our Party and since my death all the Labour Movement has been rankly abused.

GORDON.   Alas, poor party.

GHOST.   O Gordon what a falling out was there. My successor stole with juice of honeyed phrases in a vial. And in the crevices of our people's ears did pour the fatal potion. The sweet nothings of meaningless words. You too were taken in and now must pay the tax-bill for your sins.

GORDON.   But we're not taxing the rich, Ghost.

GHOST.   That's your bloody problem.

GORDON.   What will happen? Tell me?

GHOST.   Oh horrible. Horrible. Horrible. Even as we speak he plots with the Cardinal of People's Hearts.

GORDON.   What is Big Change?

GHOST.   See the yonder dawn breaks. I sink back to my world of thwarted policies, frustrated dreams and betrayed hopes. Remember me.

CHARLIE.   (Aside.) The time is out of joint. I cannot spin it right.

GORDON.   This Ghost drags me leftward and leftward. He may be the end of me yet.

SCENE TWENTY-SIX
ADVICE FROM A MENTOR

No. 10. CARDINAL and TONY-BOY. The CARDINAL is standing. TONY-BOY's cowboy boots are sticking out underneath the CARDINAL's skirt. There is a relaxed beatific expression on the CARDINAL's face. Movement below the skirt.

CARDINAL.	Hurry up Tony-Boy. Haven't you found it yet?
TONY-BOY.	Coming. Sorry Dub-Dub. (Holds up a pen.) My product-placement Mont-Blanc. Present from Chirac. Sentimental value. I'm seeing Her Majesty in thirty-seven minutes. Run it past me one more time.
CARDINAL.	Be it enacted by the Queen's most excellent Majesty, by and with the advice and consent of the Lords Spiritual and Temporal, and Commons, in the present Parliament assembled and by the authority of the same . . .
	(Puts his hand on TONY-BOY's behind.)
TONY-BOY.	This is no time for soundbites Dub-Dub. Can't you feel the hand of history?
CARDINAL.	No. A word of caution. The choice of a spin doctor in modern times is a matter of no little import. One test of a politician's wisdom is in his choice of spin doctor. You are what your spin doctor does.
TONY-BOY.	But how can one tell if they're really any good?
CARDINAL.	(Turning vicious.) Only one fail-safe method. When you discover

	that the spin doctor thinks more about himself than about you, that his actions indicate that all he seeks is to further his own miserable career, when he begins to develop airs, spends weekends with royalty, succumbs to the flattery of speculators at the Ivy restaurant, accepts hospitality in the chateaux of the Dordogne, is photographed with Hillary and Bill, then I would advise you that such a spin doctor is untrustworthy.
TONY-BOY.	How lucky I am, Dub-Dub. Polly is the exact opposite of all that.
CARDINAL.	Too many Popes have been betrayed by impetuous cardinals.
	Getting late for the Palace? A word of advice. When you're talking to Madam Windsor don't linger too long over the fiction of popular representation. Fine words butter no parsnips.
TONY-BOY.	But Dub-Dub surely they can butter some delicious scones.
CARDINAL.	No! Neither parsnips nor scones. The people are not interested in abstractions. The old Council of Ten in Venice understood this well. They had no time for piety. Nor should you.

SCENE TWENTY-SEVEN

TONY-BOY GOES DOWN THE MALL

POLLY with a microphone, like a sports commentator, speaking excitedly to the audience.

POLLY.　　　　　　　　These are the bits I love, the flashy bits, in between the dirty bits of this job. Tony-Boy, getting into the Rover limo! There he goes! Ten out of ten for the wave go the Olympic judges. Tell the party faithful to keep the union jack flying for there he goes, the carwax is gleaming, the PM is beaming, everything is seeming as we love it to seem. And for all those hundreds of disappointed and disillusioned activists leaving the party all I can say is your decision is a miracle of bad timing. My message is piss off let's flush them down the lavatory of history, 'cos Tony-Boy is just outside the Palace, gleaming and beaming and seeming and . . . (Stops.) Hey, today's not Thursday. Thursday's when he goes to see Her Majesty. Today's Monday. What the hell is going on?

(He screams. A BLACKOUT.)

SCENE TWENTY-EIGHT

CHERRY-POP alone, walking across the stage with her New Age trinkets.

CHERRY-POP.　　　　The crystal's melting! (She drops it.) The rod's too hot! (She drops it.) My idol, it's burning me! (She pulls it off and throws it away.) All the lines of power, they're overloading. It's a personal power surge. I love it. Where does power lie? In a strong man on a white mare. I know it's shameless, It's not nineties, but it is millennial. And it's US.

SCENE TWENTY-NINE
BUCK HOUSE

Buckingham Palace. TONY-BOY is waiting to be received. He appears to be learning lines. ('As First Lord of the Treasury, Ma'am it is my task to advise you . . . ') A wooden model of a single Corgi on wheels is pulled across the stage. He fingers his tie nervously. Another Corgi-on-wheels. He checks his fly is done, quickly scratches his bottom – simian behaviour. Three corgis-on-wheels. A short burst of the national anthem, followed by MRS WINDSOR in green wellies, tiara, Order of Garter on blue dress and a Barbour jacket, which she discards on entry. She is carrying secateurs which are handed to FLUNKEY.

MRS WINDSOR.	Meeting on Monday. This is unusual. We're not going to war against France are we?
TONY-BOY.	Oh no, ma'am nothing quite so adventurous.
MRS WINDSOR.	Tea or a little nip?
TONY-BOY.	Tea, please, ma'am.
MRS WINDSOR.	We will have whisky, Giovanni. He will have tea. Now dear Tony-Boy. Tell me, what is the reason for this unexpected pleasure? There haven't been more sightings of the People's Princess have there? Philip's terrified she's coming back like Elvis.
TONY-BOY.	MI6 have confirmed that the Belize sighting was a hoax. (A PAUSE.) Emotions are funny things. I had to find some when she died.
MRS WINDSOR.	I agree. Emotions do funny things to you. (Bursts into laughter.)
TONY-BOY.	Er, Yes, Ma'am. (Trying to change subject.) You've seen so much and become so wise. I'm your tenth Prime-Minister.

MRS WINDSOR.	(Frowns.) Oh dear. Are you?
TONY-BOY.	Churchill?
MRS WINDSOR.	Brandy.
TONY-BOY.	Eden?
MRS WINDSOR.	Paranoia.
TONY-BOY.	Macmillan.
MRS WINDSOR.	Charm.
TONY-BOY.	Lord Home.
MRS WINDSOR.	Defective.
TONY-BOY.	Harold Wilson.
MRS WINDSOR.	No dress-sense.
TONY-BOY.	Mr Heath.
MRS WINDSOR.	Bachelor.
TONY-BOY.	Callaghan.
MRS WINDSOR.	Policeman.
TONY-BOY.	Thatcher.
MRS WINDSOR	Mad.
TONY-BOY.	Major.
MRS WINDSOR	Tram-conductor.
TONY-BOY.	And me, ma'am.
MRS WINDSOR	Smarmy.
TONY-BOY.	Oh!
MRS WINDSOR.	(Aside.) Now do you know what it's like? This never-ending parade of second-rate men and that woman through my living room every Thursday, pretending they're actors? (To TONY-BOY.) We've been thinking, Tony-Boy, on our own, to ourselves.
TONY-BOY.	Oh, Gosh Ma'am that's good.

	That's really, really good.
MRS WINDSOR.	Ever since we lost the Empire we've been going downhill. Children in a nursery without toys. What do we say when the Sultan of Brunei asks us what Britain stands for in the world?
TONY-BOY.	You could say Ma'am that we have 286 Marks and Spencers stores in our land, collecting over a hundred million pounds a week. Tesco has branches in Poland and Hungary. Woolworths is in Belgium and our very own Argos is setting up shops in the Netherlands. And First Direct was the first telephone bank in Europe. Silent innovations, Ma'am, but wealth-creators.
MRS WINDSOR.	Oh dear, we have a fear of shop-windows. You might put us in one. The monarchy as a window-display.
TONY-BOY.	Oh no, no, Ma'am, a modern Britain needs a modern Monarchy.
MRS WINDSOR.	(Aside.) We felt a chill go down our spine. (To TONY-BOY.) Why are you really here today?
TONY-BOY.	I've come to ask you to sign an Order-in-Council dissolving Parliament.
MRS WINDSOR.	(A PAUSE.) You want new elections? With your majority? Oh how clever. You want to be re-elected with a smaller majority. Gives you a bigger margin for manoeuvre. Lord Gilmour told me over dinner last night that you were embarrassed by your majority. It stops you being as conservative as you really want.

TONY-BOY.	Exactly. (He bursts out.) That's why we want to dissolve this parliament for ever.
MRS WINDSOR.	(Shocked.) What?
TONY-BOY.	No need for concern, Ma'am. We're not ditching democracy. We're deepening it. Direct democracy.
MRS WINDSOR.	Direct?
TONY-BOY.	An annual parliament.
MRS WINDSOR.	Annual?
TONY-BOY.	Yes. It will meet once a year in the Dome on Democracy Day. Not six hundred and fifty MPs in an old-fashioned Whitehall club, but real people. 50,000 real people representing Focus Groups from every corner of your kingdom. Only they shall have the right to approve our policies.
MRS WINDSOR.	Will the House of Commons pass a Bill dissolving its own powers?
TONY-BOY.	We've tried it in the Labour Party and it works. A giant assembly of shareholders, one share one vote. One board in control, one chairman on the board. One people, one nation, one monarch.
MRS WINDSOR.	Hegemony of a somewhat dubious sort.
TONY-BOY.	(Taken aback.) Ma'am?
MRS WINDSOR.	I was at Hatchards the other day looking for a birthday present for William. A long-haired shop-assistant directed me to a book called The Modern Prince. I had it collected. Totally unsuitable for William, but strangely compulsive

	reading. Mr Gramsci was very intelligent. He talks a great deal of hegemony but not in your way.
TONY-BOY.	(Panicking.) No, Ma'am.
MRS WINDSOR.	He says that the capitalist state and the specific characteristics of the class struggle make it possible for several politically dominant classes or fractions to function.
TONY-BOY.	(Doesn't understand.) All we're going to do is to put the people in the Dome.
MRS WINDSOR.	Exactly. But which fraction amongst them will be hegemonic?
TONY-BOY.	None of them. No 10 will set the agenda and . . .
MRS WINDSOR.	Hegemonically tell everyone what to do. You have a problem Tony-Boy. If you dissolve Parliament, who will raise taxes, control the money?
TONY-BOY.	Oh, the Inland Revenue Focus Group will be vested with these powers, Ma'am.
MRS WINDSOR.	(Threatening but flirtatious.) What if I don't sign?
TONY-BOY.	(Threatening but flirtatious.) Charles would.
MRS WINDSOR.	Would he? Yes he would. He'd love it.
TONY-BOY.	You've got to sign. You're a Constitutional Monarch.
MRS WINDSOR.	I've got to sign. I'm a Constitutional Monarch.
	(She signs.)

TONY-BOY.	Permission to take your leave Ma'am. And if you allow me I'll return this volume to Hatchards. There's been a terrible mistake.
MRS WINDSOR.	(Nods.) Would your wife like some curly broccoli from our garden? It's not organic like Charles's broccoli.
	(They stare at each other.)
TONY-BOY.	Good-night Ma'am.
	(He EXITS.)
MRS WINDSOR.	Philip! We might have to live in Canada.

SCENE THIRTY

GORDON, dishevelled, wanders across the stage.

GORDON.	I might have to go and live in Scotland. Cheer up, Gordon. Lead the party in Scotland. Win the Highland Games. Toss the caber of liberty on Westminster's decaying head. Guide my hand, Kier Hardie, and save me from the corrupting influence of wealth. (HE PAUSES.) Yes, I am going to do this.

SCENE THIRTY-ONE

BIG CHANGE – YOU KNOW IT MAKES SENSE

Outside No.10. Media, flashing cameras, etc. TONY-BOY walks out to thunderous applause.

TONY-BOY.	(Starts with fake humility.) A new dawn has broken. After an all-night sitting the Democracy Bill went

through the House and was immediately approved by the Lords, consisting last night exclusively of newly ennobled theatre and film directors.

OK, but, you know it's you, the people that really count. One Britain. That is the patriotism of the future. When a business is in distress we all suffer . Suffer together or succeed together. We are now today the people's parliament. A parliament of all the people. As President Clinton once said and this is an exact quote: 'There is no one more powerful than a member of the focus group. If you really want to change things that's where you want to be.' And you know, we are all focus groups now. It's really over to you. I know what you're thinking. What about human nature. What if anti-social elements enter the Focus Groups to distort their meaning. Our written Constitution has an answer written into it by the Cardinal. Plebiscitary democracy. Referenda. You can have one a year. But if the need arises, three a year or one every month or every week or every day or two a day one on the Today programme and one on Newsnight who've both gone digital. So no probs. B-Sky-B are fitting devices in every home to facilitate democracy. You can vote as easily as you flick a channel. Do it every day. Register your view. Do it every hour, every minute. Every second. In the end you won't notice what you're choosing. Pure, direct, democracy. It'll become part of everyday life like the shopping. Like the parking. And we'll make sure that the country runs well. Goodbye old. Think new. Let me give you an example of old thinking. Three hundred of you have written me a letter asking me to renationalise the railways because you feel they're dirty and unsafe. But there are 800,000 members of the Royal Society for the Protection of Birds. Three hundred or 800,000. It's obvious isn't it? We don't want elitism in our country. I'm going back into No.10 now and . . . (Pointing.) . . . There in that office you'll see my light on all night. You'll know I'm doing my best for you. God bless you. Rule Britannia.

(He EXITS.)

SCENE THIRTY-TWO

THE NARRATIVE OF YOUR LIFE HAS TO BE REARRANGED

Spinners on stage at either end.

POLLY. The Big Change referendum. It was the spin of my life. John O'Groats turned round to where Land's End is. Was.

(She gyrates, singing.)

O round and round and round I go
Whichever way the wind doth blow
Like a top I spin and spin
Doing all my enemies.

(She stops, breathless.)

CHARLIE. Cut the crap, Polly. Tell them. Tell them how many voted.

POLLY.	(Very fast talk.) Turnout doesn't matter. All that matters is win-win and we won-won. We won the Big One. (Aside.) We will.
	(POLLY's phone rings.)
	Where are you ringing from? Scotland? Have they found him. Oh no. (Spins.) Fine. Fine. Don't send any grouse, Tony-Boy's gone vegetarian.
CHARLIE.	(Aside.) Big Change? Big Win? The story is the roads to Scotland are jammed. Mercenaries have been sent to Hadrian's Wall. Gordon is moving from croft to croft at night. And now, safe at last, he basks in the loch with Salmon. To Scotland I shall go. Must get the accent sorted.
	(A curtain is pulled back revealing a tableau from Braveheart with GORDON as Wallace.)
GORDON.	(Aside.) Highland spring water. Highland air. A display of appalling goalkeeping at Ibrox Park. A tree of liberty. Is it too late? I still Bonny Prince with indecision.
	(Enter GHOST.)
	Is it too late? Has someone else done the thing that was to be done? O cursed fate that ever I was sent to put this right.
GHOST.	To thy brother Salmon go. Lead him to the Scottish TUC and there will rebellion grow.

SCENE THIRTY-THREE

LAST PRAYER, LAST ORDERS, LIGHTS OUT

POLLY comes on. Aside.

POLLY.   That's your lot. Democracy once a year for an afternoon. Life without politics, politics without enemies and you should all be bloody grateful and get out there and vote for our referendums.

A few ground rules for leaving this theatre. People of Scottish origin please observe there is a curfew in force as you leave this theatre. Do not walk in groups of more than two. People of any origin, fleeing to Scotland, will not be able to travel on Heaven trains. Coaches to Glasgow and Edinburgh can only be boarded outside the Dome, where security cameras can record your eye-balls.

A special Heaven commuter train with free champagne and a smoked-salmon night-cap has been laid on for all those returning to Surrey. But as you prepare to leave for the comfort of home and public house, observe.

(Suddenly the stage goes dark. A window is lit.)

Our leader works for us through the long night.

(The cast come on and kneel, pointing to the window. TONY-BOY leans out and gives a modest wave.)

TONY-BOY.   No, no please. Stop. Thank you, gosh. It's a personal thing, religion, but I don't think people would mind if we ended with a prayer. The New Lord's prayer. (TONY-BOY leads the prayer. It is shown on the heading display above the stage.)

Our country which art in Europe
Hallowed be thy investments
Thy profits come, Thy dividends increase
in Wall Street and Far East.
Give us this day influence in Washington
And do not let the Germans displace us.
Forgive us our bad debts as we do not forgive those who are indebted to us.
Save us from the nightmares of Old Labour
And deliver us from the trades-unions.
For Capital rules Britannia
And always will.
Amen. Mammon.

THE END.

APPENDIX
TO BE READ AT YOUR PERIL
OFF-MESSAGE SOUNDBITES
FROM OLD LABOUR TRAITORS

DEBASED PRESS

'The most desperate attempts are being made to popularise the coming Coronation. Public authorities have been given power to spend the rate-payers' money illegally on decorations and festivities. Poor little half-starved children are to be presented with Coronation mugs or medals to commemorate the event . . .

Thus, despite all the efforts of astute stage-managers, royalty is being found out. It is a huge imposture. The atmosphere of the court is surcharged with hypocrisy, insincerity, flattery and immorality . . . Half a century ago Republicanism was the creed of Radicalism and Nonconformity. But the corrupting influences of wealth and a debased newspaper press have eaten the soul out of the nation . . . '

Keir Hardie, 1910

THE IDOLATRY OF WEALTH

' . . . The quality in modern societies, which is most sharply opposed to the teaching ascribed to the Founder of the Christian Faith, lies deeper than the exceptional failures and abnormal follies against which criticism is most commonly directed. It consists in the assumption, accepted by most reformers with hardly less naivete than by the defenders of the established order, that the attainment of material riches is the supreme object of human endeavour and the final criterion of human success. Such a philosophy, plausible, militant, and not indisposed, when hard pressed, to silence criticism by persecution, may triumph or decline. What is certain is that it is the negation of any sytstem of thought or morals which can, except by a metaphor, be described as Christian.'

R.H. Tawney, 1926

GREAT CHANGES

'The Labour Party stands for such great changes in the economic and social structure that it cannot function successfully unless it obtains a majority which is prepared to put its principles into practice. Those principles are so far-reaching that they affect every department of of the public services and every phase of policy. The plain fact is that a Socialist Party cannot hope to make a success of administering the Capitalist system because it does not believe in it.'

Clement Atlee, 'The Labour Party in Perspective', 1936

LET US FACE THE FUTURE

' . . . In the years that followed, the 'hard-faced men' and their political friends kept control of the government. They controlled the banks, the mines, the big industries, largely the press and the cinema. They controlled the means by which people got their living. They controlled the ways by which most of the people learned about the world outside. This happened in all the industrialised countries.

Great economic blizzards swept the world in those years. The great inter-war slumps were not acts of God or blind forces. They were the sure and certain result of the concentration of too much economic power in the hands of too few men. These men had only learned how to act in the interest of their own bureaucratically run private monopolies which may be likened to totalitarian oligarchies within our democratic state.

They had and felt no responsibility to the nation. Similar forces are at work today . . . '

Labour Party election manifesto, 1945

MIXED ECONOMY

'We should make two things clear: . . . we have no intention of abandoning public ownership and that we regard public ownership not as an end in itself but as a means to certain ends . . . While we shall certainly wish to extend public ownership, . . . our goal is not 100% state ownership. Our goal is a society in which Socialist ideals are realised . . . The pace at which we can go depends on how quickly we can persuade our fellow citizens to back us.'

Hugh Gaitskell, Labour Party Conference, Blackpool, 1959

SPECULATORS

'A financial speculator can clear a million pounds overnight on a property deal buying and selling a block of flats with somebody else's money and that is smart business; but if you pay a decent wage to the engine driver or a miner that is raging inflation. The banks can lend tens of millions to the Stock Exchange speculators and that is highly consonant with the national interest; but local authorities trying to cope with their heritage of slums or with tragic and heartrending overcrowding are forced into costly borrowing operations at penal rates of interest . . . Are they going to say a Socialist party is irrelevant to these problems?'

Harold Wilson, Labour Party conference speech, 1960

FULL EMPLOYMENT

'Next year will be the 50th anniversary of the 1944 White Paper on Employment. That White Paper said: 'The

Government accept as one of their primary aims and responsibilities the maintenance of a high and stable level of employment'. Today, I reaffirm that aim. The goal of full employment remains right at the heart of Labour's vision for Britain'.

John Smith, speech to the Trade Union Congress, 1993